CW00540862

Praise for
Midlife: Stories of crisis and grow

While developing my own research on the embodied experience of post-menopause, it became clear to me that there is a scarcity of psychotherapeutic literature looking at the existential experience of midlife. Helen Kewell has sought to fill that gap, and achieves it beautifully. Writing as a midlife therapist herself, Kewell wisely avoids the all-good, all-bad dichotomy embraced by too many contemporary writers on this life phase, instead offering a nuanced and thoughtful account of work with midlife clients in supervision and in her own therapy. Gratifyingly, she also acknowledges that much recent focus has been limited far too often to the menopausal transition of white, cisgender, middle-class women. Including thinking on working with men, queer people, and Black and minoritised clients, she offers a book that might support all of us to better attend to the work we co-create with people within and without the mainstream narrative.

Dr Stella Duffy, psychotherapist, author and researcher

Midlife can seem like a daunting time of crisis, but Helen Kewell's book will take you on an adventurous journey through the wilderness of midlife transitions. Whether you are a practitioner or someone poised at this cusp of life, this book will open your eyes to the possibilities and opportunities that are on offer, especially if you are in search of understanding and want to learn more about the meaning of human existence.

Professor Emmy van Deurzen, Founder/Director of the Existential Academy, psychologist, existential psychotherapist and author

Helen Kewell artfully weaves personal experience, therapeutic dialogue and lived experience with scientific knowledge, psychological theories, contemporary commentary and existential philosophy in her exploration of the midlife. Each chapter focuses on a different element of the experience and Helen looks at how this phase of life impacts work, the experience of the body, sex, sexuality and intimate relationships and the process of ageing and gaining wisdom. She guides you through the inevitable layers of the experience and leaves you with a greater understanding of this often-overlooked period of human life. Written in an accessible way, it is ideal for anyone interested in the topic and essential reading for therapists wishing to gain a deeper understanding of clients who are currently in or facing this stage of life.

Dr Claire Arnold-Baker, Principal, New School of Psychotherapy and Counselling, and counselling psychologist, existential psychotherapist and author

We are learning to take the stigma out of seeking help with our mindsets but we still have a long way to go. Mix this with the hormonal changes we all experience in midlife – it's amazing that we don't see more people reaching crisis point at this time. This book is an excellent exploration of being human and making the most of midlife, of not allowing the past to dictate how we live in the future. I love the way Helen Kewell uses examples from her own work to show just how normal it is to talk to someone outside our 'inner circles' and make good use of it for us and those around us. She is very human herself, and this in itself makes her and those like her much more accessible. I also like her approach to the body being a great guide to how we are really feeling. I hope the book encourages more people to seek out the many huge benefits talking therapy can give.

Sally Gunnell OBE, health and wellbeing coach

About the author

Helen Kewell is a humanistic counsellor and supervisor with a private practice in Sussex. She is the author of *Living Well and Dying Well: Tales of counselling older people* (also published by PCCS Books (2019)) and is a regular contributor to *BACP Workplace* journal and *Therapy Today* on the topics of life transitions and ageing. Inspired by existential approaches to life, she advocates that major life transitions can be as revealing as they are painful if navigated with patience and curiosity. Helen is also an educator in counselling and wellbeing and a management consultant specialising in people and organisational change.

MidLife

Stories of crisis
and growth from
the counselling room

HELEN KEWELL

First published 2024

PCCS Books Ltd
Wyastone Business Park
Wyastone Leys
Monmouth
NP25 3SR
UK

Tel +44 (0)1600 891509
contact@pccs-books.co.uk
www.pccs-books.co.uk

Midlife: Stories of crisis and growth from the counselling room

British Library Cataloguing in Publication Data.
A catalogue record for this book is available from the British Library

ISBNs:
paperback – 978 1 915220 49 3
epub – 978 1 915220 50 9

Cover design by Jason Anscomb
Printed in the UK by TJ Books, Padstow, Cornwall.

Dedication

To the small but mighty army of friends with whom I travel this life, and to my sister, Sarah, who bravely faced into the headwind of crisis and, miraculously, came out resplendent.

Midlife

Stories of crisis and growth from the counselling room

Contents

Acknowledgements

Over the past year, I have had the privilege of talking to many different people specifically about their midlife experiences. I want to thank them for gifting me their time and perspectives so generously. I hope I have done them justice.

Throughout writing this book, I have also been on my own journey into midlife, and my quietly brilliant counsellor continues to hold space for me to explore this. I am so grateful to her, not only for this but also for showing me the art of the possible, which inspires my own practice.

I am grateful as ever to my mum, Anne, for tirelessly proofreading every word before I dare to send it to my editor, and for knowing enough about counselling theory (and me) to gently challenge me. And to Catherine, for being simply the most honest (ouch) and meticulously detailed editor and making me the best version of my printed self.

This book was written while working full time and I want to say a big thank you to my husband, Nick, and our three almost-grown-up children, for their patience and for the supplies of hot drinks, food and encouragement while I tapped at my keyboard at weekends and in the evenings, drowning in notes and books, hardly noticing their presence.

Last, being able to work as a counsellor is never something I take for granted. The clients I have worked with through my career to date have taught me more about life than any other experience or book ever has. I am grateful for the trust they have placed in me that makes that all possible.

Foreword

My mother was born during the time of Empire and came to the United Kingdom as part of the Windrush generation, her flight from the Caribbean borne on the wings of hope that she would be accepted as British and the belief that she was coming 'home'. When I was in my late teens, I would often return to the house to find my mother, who was by then in her late 40s, sat in front of the television watching the American talk show host Oprah Winfrey. One of Oprah's phrases to which she would often nod knowingly was 'Turn your wounds into wisdom' – a phrase I would hear her occasionally muttering to herself in the days afterwards.

Life for my mother was difficult; she endured racism, sexism and other hatreds both outside the home and inside, meaning that it was only in her midlife that she started to find herself – then it was that, as Oprah had suggested, she learned from her wounds. Rejecting Catholicism to take a more Baptist religious leaning was just one of the ways forward for my mother, as she learned from the pain of her past and was able to create a better, more authentic future for herself.

This is why this book resonated so much for me. It offers a positive and incredibly powerful pathway forward for those whose midlife stories have maybe been lost in the socially constructed mayhem of modernity and the oppressiveness that others, and so silences, older voices, and particularly the voices of older women. Books such as this should be essential reading for counsellors, psychotherapists and anyone else in the helping professions. It speaks to such an important stage of our life and development, be we practitioners or clients. I know from personal professional experience that, of the clients I have the pleasure to work with, a good number will present with some kind of life crisis around midlife. It may be a crisis of confidence in the workplace as they witness a younger generation join their workforce and succeed them, or an existential angst as they watch their children leave home to build their own lives. And this is what inspires me in Helen Kewell's book. Midlife, as she presents it here, is the pivot for a shift in perspective from who we were to who we might yet be. It is a message of growth, of hope.

This book is an intricate mapping of the shedding of the performative and stereotypical, socially constructed roles of gender, race, colour, culture and sexuality, and the progression, hopefully, to a more authentic self – a self that, in its intersectional authenticity, acts less like it is supposed to, preferring instead to live more like it desires to.

And, as with the stories of growth and wisdom held in this book, this was for me the beauty of watching my mother become more the woman she wanted to be. This was the lesson she taught her son, the man writing this foreword, who is himself now in his midlife.

Dwight Turner, PhD.
Dwight leads the Humanistic Counselling and Psychotherapy course at the University of Brighton. He is a psychotherapist and supervisor in private practice, and author of books including *The Psychology of Supremacy* (2023) and *Intersections of Privilege and Otherness in Counselling and Psychotherapy* (2021).

Introduction
We need to talk about midlife

She is climbing her own mountain, in search of her own
horizon, after years of being absorbed in the struggles of others.
The way is hard, she stumbles many times, but for once no one
is scrambling after her, begging her to turn back. The air grows
thin, and she may often feel dizzy. Sometimes the weariness
spreads from her aching bones to her heart and brain, but she
knows that when she has scrambled up this last sheer obstacle,
she will see how to handle the rest of her long life.
Germaine Greer, *The Change* (1991/2018, pp.386–387)

He's a man… riding on a smile and the shoeshine. And when
they start not smiling back, that's an earthquake.
Arthur Miller, *Death of a Salesman* (1949/2015, p.111)

We read about, hear about and often create gross caricatures of
midlife. For women and men alike, it is generally presented as a point
of crisis, marked for women by the menopause and the end of their
fertility; for men, by a last flourish of virility. It is often characterised
by feelings and behaviours that are extreme or out of character. And
it is generally assumed to be followed by a slow, inevitable slide into
irrelevancy and increasing disability.

Despite a rapidly increasing volume of rhetoric in recent years
about longevity and positive ageing, the prevailing narrative remains

that we accelerate and flourish through our younger-to-mid life, and then decline gradually towards our death. Midlife originated as a concept in the 1950s as life expectancy began to increase rapidly, due to advances in healthcare and the cessation of the mass killings of two world wars. No wonder there was a rhetoric of existential crisis: what were we to do with this extra life time afforded to us?

According to the World Economic Forum, average global life expectancy is now 71.7 years (2023). In the UK, it is around 80 years, depending on your gender at birth (Office for National Statistics, 2021). Most of us in our mid-50s can expect another 30 to 40 years of living in this new, post-midlife/menopausal version of ourselves. The reality is that, as we find ourselves in this midlife transition, it is disorientating. Our sense of self, our body and the world around us, which is always changing, moves past some invisible tolerance level, and suddenly we wonder who we are. Yet, while this takes some adjusting to, transitions offer us rich potential to move into a new space. So, let's turn the midlife narrative on its head. Let's all open ourselves up to ageing consciously and positively – across our whole lives.

Gail Sheehy, who writes tirelessly on life transitions, takes a positive spin on midlife. She calls this phase of life 'the Second Adulthood' (the Flourishing Forties and Flaming Fifties, indeed!), where we move from the Age of Mastery into the Age of Integrity (1995). She describes a colourful landscape full of dips and peaks, as well as internal crises around our mortality and meaning and purpose. This depiction of an unpredictable yet adventurous landscape feels very real to me. Abraham Maslow (1968), along with Carl Rogers (1961), maintained that human beings are always motivated towards leading a fuller life and living deeply authentically, to the best of our potential and circumstances, and that this journey, inevitably, takes us through crisis, tragedy and pain, as well as through times of joy. This grittily real but broadly hopeful viewpoint resonates with me. So too does the existential philosophy of thinkers such as Jean Paul Sartre and Simone de Beauvoir, which calls on us to face into the realities of life while also encouraging us to live fully and authentically. I would argue that we are never more vibrantly forced into authenticity than when we come face to face with our mortality in the transition process of midlife.

But how well prepared are we as a society to respond to this life stage? Can we create a world where the turbulence of the midlife experience is witnessed and explored in service of people's growth? Can public and professional consciousness conceive of midlife as a time of regeneration as well as loss, of liberation as well as dependency? Certainly, in my own profession of counselling and psychotherapy, we still have a limited narrative about the menopause in particular – even though up to 62% of the members of BACP, the main professional association representing some 65,000 practitioners, are likely to be in midlife and therefore menopausal (Bodza et al., 2019). There is clearly a need for greater acknowledgement and deeper understanding about the menopause here, on both a professional and personal level (Anderson & Posner, 2002). And more generally, in society as a whole, much is being missed without this open acknowledgement of and dialogue about the challenges and growth opportunities of the menopause and midlife within friendship groups, families and the workplace, and among health and mental health practitioners.

My indignation at this negative paradigm is fuelled by the very different lived reality I encountered in my counselling work with older adult clients, which inspired my first book (Kewell, 2019), *Living Well and Dying Well*. This focused on the specific crises but also the opportunities for growth in the later, final stages of life, revealed through stories from the counselling room. I now feel compelled to look at midlife through this same reframing lens.

According to research, approximately 13 million women in the UK are currently either peri- or post-menopausal (Nuffield Health, 2021/2023). It is estimated that, by 2030, there will be more than 1.2 billion menopausal women worldwide, with 47 million entering the menopause annually (Birmingham, 2021), in a process lasting on average around 15 years. When we also consider that employment rates have risen fastest among women aged 55–64, clearly these are statistics none of us can ignore (Francis-Devine & Hutton, 2024). It becomes compelling from a therapeutic perspective when we understand that more than 60% of menopausal women experience symptoms resulting in behaviour changes, almost half say they feel depressed, a third say they suffer with anxiety and a great many also report feeling as though they are 'going mad'. Strikingly, approximately two thirds of women say there is a general lack of support and understanding for what they are going through (Menopause Support, 2022). At the same time, our life events stack up: children mature and leave home; our partners face their own midlife, and often existential, challenges; our careers peak; our parents become dependent on us or die. We are each a story that is always unfolding. In existential philosophy, true authenticity involves facing up to the inevitable truth of our own finitude and living each moment as vital components of a story. (Inevitably, as a woman in the perimenopausal phase herself, I will write collectively as 'we' from time to time when referring to the female experience of menopause.)

The increasing amount of coverage that the menopause and midlife are receiving in the media and in daily conversations is a welcome and radical shift in the past few years. In 2022, the cross-party parliamentary Women and Equalities Committee called on the UK government to amend the Equality Act to introduce menopause as a protected characteristic, and to include a duty on employers to provide reasonable adjustments for menopausal employees. Although this campaign has not yet achieved its goal, the lobbying continues. Even as I write, the dialogue will have moved on. This heightened level of public and private awareness can only help to reduce the feelings of isolation and shame that midlife crises and the symptoms of menopause can create. It is so welcome.

And men's experiences in midlife may be equally negative. Emerging research is showing that the generation of men who are now entering midlife feel displaced and less sure of their purpose (Reeves, 2022). Poor mental health is prevalent among middle-aged men in many if not most Westernised societies, regardless of whether they continue to retain their gendered power, wealth and status. A detailed longitudinal study by the mental health and suicide prevention charity Samaritans showed that men in the UK and Ireland are three to four times more likely than women to die by suicide and that those who are living on low incomes in the most deprived areas are most at risk (2020). Similarly, in the US, pre-pandemic studies found that middle-aged men tend to be more reluctant to seek help for or discuss feelings of low mood, and to take greater health risks, leading to a suicide completion rate four times higher than that among women (Berman & McNelis, 2017). Both reports point to factors such as exclusion from an evolving job market, changing male gender norms, relationship issues and social isolation as the causes of this.

And while menopause impacts 100% of people with ovaries, this doesn't of course always signify only those who identify as female. Until relatively recently, the medical model for the menopause, and the prevailing narrative, have been those of white men, and seen through the lens of 'not male' rather than a female or non-gendered frame. Moreover, most people providing public, mainstream perspectives, while they have definitively increased political and public awareness of the issue, are white, middle-class, straight women – among them, Davina McCall, Mariella Fostrup, Caitlin Moran and Dr Louise Newson. I am also one of them – I am part of this problem, if you like. We do have to clear the way for a more open conversation about midlife across all intersections of gender association, race and social groups. People along those lines of intersection – people of colour, those who are queer, those in poverty, those who are gender diverse – are likely already to feel marginalised and overlooked, and possibly be experiencing multiple micro-aggressions in social and healthcare settings that further complicate their lived experience of menopause. The effect of this is summed up brilliantly by psychotherapist and writer Tania Glyde in their research on queer menopause: '[This] confers on the individual a very specific form of structural stigma' (2023) and can lead to people failing to seek what could be lifesaving medical support and, likewise, counselling.

Four years ago, at the age of 45, I took myself back into personal therapy. The trigger was, on the surface, nebulous; I was almost surprised to be there. My new counsellor was also female and in midlife – not a conscious choice on my part (yet not unusual, given the demographics of our profession). As we settled into our chairs in her sun-flooded room, she invited me to begin wherever I would like, but in a way that allowed me to sit for a while in the warmth of her welcome and let something surface. I watched as a robin hop-hopped along the low brick wall on the patio and settled onto a garden ornament, cocked its head at me and then flew off. The words that came out of my mouth were: 'Well, my eldest niece turns 18 in December, and I suppose I am realising that this phase of life, the childhood years, are coming to an end.' My counsellor nodded but I was startled: where did that spring from? A wise friend, herself battling with the menopause, once told me that, while her physical symptoms hit her like a brick wall, she could now see that midlife, and menopause itself, creeps insidiously into our lives, with no resounding alarms. And here it was for me, slithering into my consciousness.

Thankfully I had already navigated myself into a counselling relationship. Over the course of the next two years, we worked through the process of finding 'me', sometimes unearthing new parts of myself, sometimes simply witnessing as other parts careered into our consciousness with a trumpet salute. The process was as painful as it was beautiful.

Midlife should be seen as a time of regeneration and revolution of self, as well as one of loss; a time of liberation as well as growing acceptance of dependency. By bringing a deep understanding of the landscape of midlife and menopause (developmentally, emotionally and physically), we counsellors can listen in, witness and help our clients navigate this intense, complex time of their lives. We can provide a safe space to explore their myriad physical and emotional 'symptoms' in service of their growth. But how do we make sure we don't inadvertently silence those we work with? Or homogenise them with clumsy generalisations or our own internal filters? After all, midlife, as with every other experience, is an entirely unique encounter for each of us.

There are countless self-help books on the menopause – mainly on the individual physical experience or dealing with broad emotional themes through a semi-autobiographical frame. It isn't my ambition to write another. There are still woefully few about male midlife. And there are far fewer, if any, that specifically inform how counselling and other helping professionals can actively support and enhance the midlife stage, or indeed how we can support each other. Our own human experience is intimately connected to others; we are nothing without the inter-relational space around us; this is how we make sense of the world, ourselves and our place within it. Our existence is only existence in the world with others (Heidegger, 1927/2010). As counsellors, carers, helpers, friends and family members, we don't simply journey alongside or observe those we meet who are grappling with midlife; we are *part of it with them*. I was lucky to have a counsellor who understood and actively entered into that maelstrom with me, and I am blessed with friends who also walk these paths (sometimes literally, accompanied by our dogs) and help me make sense of it.

My existential and humanistic orientation as a counselling practitioner means I have a naturally philosophical outlook on life and towards my counselling work. It is a way of being in the world that is embodied, in the present moment, curious and exacting. It is from this perspective that I explore the stories and experiences in this book. I believe that we must live with purpose and stay fully immersed in all the realities, crises and dilemmas of existence, even if life is painful, as many midlife experiences can be. The truth of life, such as it is, reveals itself through this immersion, and this knowledge then allows us to live freely, or at least with full awareness. Of course, we can't 'make it better' by revealing what is happening and how we feel, but we can understand ourselves and our reality somewhat better. This invariably involves exploring our past and present and imagining our future, and making sense of these three as a system, a map of our own experience.

The great existentialists understood this and wrote prolifically and vividly about it. Simone de Beauvoir, in particular, found her midlife and approaching old age a painful experience. She (1970/1972) encouraged us in her writings to maintain a strong relationship with our core sense of self, even while others around us seek to commandeer our outward expression of who we are in the world. Always unflinching in dealing in life's realities, Jean-Paul Sartre wrote that, if we can't find freedom in ageing due to its inevitability, we can create our own freedom in the meaning we bestow on the process as we face into it (1956/2003). In a wonderful summary of this existential attitude to the ageing process, psychiatrist Chris Gilleard concluded that our task is 'balancing the weight of the past with the weightlessness of the future to forge an authentic present' (2022, p.290). I rather like the idea of this weightlessness of the future, as it implies possibility and optionality.

I believe that, for all of us to achieve a sense of fulfilment and wellbeing, we can and should attend to mind, body and spirit, as well as to the social and relational spaces around us. This 'whole-person' approach to living a full life is essential. Talking therapy is hugely supportive and can very much be a healing space, but practitioners of any health and welfare discipline do the people we work with a disservice if we don't hold a broad and varied awareness of what else will support their wellbeing. One of the reasons for writing this book is to help educate all practitioners about the psychological and emotional landscape of midlife transition, in addition to helping counsellors have a full and wide perspective on the topic. Midlife, along with many life transitions, is a transition for our whole body and self. For this reason, I have conducted research and considered broad perspectives from healthcare practitioners, nutritional therapists and physical therapists too. There are many resources available to us now.

Psychotherapy is a powerful driver for social change, at both a macro and a micro level. As practitioners, it is our responsibility to seek to understand our clients' experiences of racism, ageism, sexism and misogyny in their lives and to act in ways that neutralise the toxicity of such experience. The rich landscape of midlife can be powerfully explored in counselling, but it can also be revealed on a walk with a friend, in frank conversations with loved ones or in a chance conversation with a stranger on a bus. I hope to show how the gifts of existential enquiry from within the counselling frame can help us move through the maelstrom of midlife and menopause and into our second adulthood.

I have woven psychological and counselling theory, research and philosophy with wider conversations with wise minds in the field to create fictionalised stories based on my reflections from my own practice. All these stories are offered as 'real' but have been blended and anonymised to protect the confidentiality of those who have shared their experience with me. I use these anecdotes as gateways to conversations that all of us can have with ourselves and those that journey through life with us: friends, colleagues, family members, helping professionals. My hope is that the book will provide perspective and inspiration and provoke reflection in all who read it that will enrich your own thinking, practice and life, and that of those around you.

A note on terminology

I have included as many voices and perspectives on midlife as I have been able to source, from first-hand, published and reported accounts, but there are others who have done this far better than me and in far more detail. Tania Glyde's work on queer menopause (2023) and Heather Corinna's representation of an inclusive menopause (2021) are both worth a deep dive.

Where I use the term 'women' or 'woman', I am referring to those who were assigned female at birth and who identify as female. Where I use the term 'men' or 'man', I am referring to those assigned male at birth and who identify as male. I use the terms trans-female or trans-male for those who have transitioned to the opposite gender from that assigned to them at birth. I use gender-diverse as a more general term for those who are not cis-gender. I have aimed to be vigilant for heteronormative narratives and to reflect a diversity of race, class, gender and age in the voices and experiences I've reported in these pages.

Chapter 1
Midlife – crisis?

Transition is a vital period of adjustment, creativity and rebirth that helps one find meaning.
There is an odd safety in this time. There is purpose.
Bruce Feiler, *Life is in the Transitions* (2021, pp.143,155)

To become wise, you must learn to listen to the wild dogs barking in your cellar.
Irvin D. Yalom, *Staring at the Sun* (2008, p.211)

In the almost dark of a blustery, angry winter mid-morning, the overhead light and a valiant candle were doing little to bring the warmth of light into my counselling room. Shedding her coat and declining my offer of a blanket, Jane settled into her chair, folded her hands into her lap and sighed.

'Ah… that felt like a sigh that needed to come out,' I said.

'I feel like I've been holding that in all week!' she exclaimed.

I waited for more to come, just affirming what she had said with a nod.

'Nothing feels definitive, or solid and I suppose everything feels possible and impossible all at once,' she went on.

'Hmmm. That feels tiring, and perhaps confusing, the way you describe it.' I tried to validate what she had said and get closer to how it felt from her experience.

'Yes.' Jane frowned slightly; there was a frustrated clip to her voice, her eyes moving away from mine, focused on nothing in particular.

'And is this particularly related to home or to work, I wonder?' We had been exploring new career options, playing with the idea of semi-retirement or a refocus.

'They all feel connected in a way. I suppose that is part of the confusion?'

This last comment came as a question, so I checked with Jane if confusion was the right word for what she was feeling. It was, so I continued: 'And this *confusion*, as you bring it here today, where is it settling in your body, what are you experiencing?'

She paused for a beat, looked up and wrinkled her face a little to concentrate inwards.

'I feel heavy, I suppose, like it is sitting low in my abdomen,' and she unfolded her hands to place her palms on her stomach. 'But it is also fizzing – no, more like buzzing. It has this infuriating energy to it. Which is annoying because I am tired today and I need to rest but I don't feel I can be at peace.'

'You don't feel at peace,' I repeated and paused.

'Yeah… no,' Jane replied.

Jane had been coming for counselling with me for more than two years, initially to explore her experience of chronic ill health – she'd been diagnosed with lupus in 2012. Outwardly confident and articulate, with a warmth to her voice, she gave an impression of inner strength that radiated outwards, almost out of her awareness. She had risen through a career in the legal profession, topping out in a place of authority that signified her deep expertise, and held a strong connection to her purpose. This love of her job, and the belief that she was doing good, gave her a true sense of inner wellbeing, with which she was able connect and from this draw strength, even when her illness was flaring up and she felt low.

She was in her early 50s, with two children born early in her marriage and two further children, siblings, adopted in their early years. Fierce and loving, ready to battle for her children, who now ranged in age from their late teens to late 20s, Jane proudly described the strong boundaries and principles she cultivated in the way she parented them. Her marriage was a constant in her life, but also a frequent source of frustration. Having pretty much taken independent paths emotionally, she and her husband were more like joint family facilitators than intimate partners.

Jane's chronic ill health, brought on by birth trauma with her first child, was forcing her to make choices about her career and to spend more time at home, often alone, which prompted introspection and unearthed a feeling of profound regret. This was further complicated by the confluence with being menopausal. With her condition, it was very hard to know which symptoms belonged to menopause, which to lupus and which to something else. The treatment and medication were complicated and her ongoing discussions with doctors were vital and maddening in equal measure. These physical and biological factors brought an otherwise externally focused and driven woman into a stark recognition of both her physical limitations and her internal experience. It also slowed life and time down a little and a tiny chink was opening to something not yet named. This was what prompted her to seek counselling. Who was she now? What would she do next, be next? Would her relationship survive?

If we examine the language used most frequently in relation to midlife, it often implies humans are either victims of it or somehow trying to avoid or overcome it. We hear words such as struggle, suffer, crisis, mastery and meltdown, and a copious use of medical terminology describing specific symptomatology and biology – hot flushes and brain fog for menopausal women, and low libido and reduced muscle mass in men. All of this implies, first, that we are largely passive participants in this transition and, second, that it is something to be subdued, overcome or healed. In so many ways, midlife is none of these things. As the writer and feminist Germaine Greer said of ageing, 'I can't see the point of battling against it when you know the outcome can only be defeat' (1991/2018, p.10). Greer expresses here both the inevitability of the ageing journey and the concept of midlife as a transition that we move through, rather than merely an unpleasant event to be survived or an enemy to be subdued.

Indeed, put simply, most of life is a transition from one state or phase to another – often revealing, frequently painful. We move from childhood to adolescence, dependence to independence, youth to older age, childhood to parenthood. We pass through relationships; we move home, change jobs, experience loss; we may transition across genders. We are indeed fluent in transitioning, but perhaps we have just never thought of our experience that way. This is expressed so beautifully by writer and anti-ageism campaigner Ashton Applewhite (2017): 'Aging is not a problem to be fixed or a disease to be cured. It is a natural, powerful, lifelong process that unites us all.'

Even the terminology reflects how midlife for women is perceived. In the Western, industrialised world, women have learned to expect, even fear, the 'climacteric' (as it was traditionally known in more academic circles) or the 'change' (a common Western euphemism, implying threat, not promise). But in China, it is rather wonderfully known as the 'second spring'. And in indigenous cultures, older women look forward to the end of their labour-intense, child-rearing years, and take their place as elders and carers with pride.

Let's get down to basics. Midlife (or middle age) is generally seen as being between 40 and 65 years of age. This might surprise those of us who assume that 50 would be the milestone marker, and it will of course vary, depending on where you live in the world and what the life expectancy is. Setting actual age range aside, midlife is a phase that we all move through, between early adulthood and older life. One man that I spoke to when researching this book, who had just turned 40, felt that he came through his own midlife transition in his mid-to-late 30s, following the death of one of his parents and coinciding with becoming a father. 'I was lost in grief and felt the drudgery of being a father,' he told me. 'My life had become something to "get through". Once I reconnected to my "self" through the process of counselling, I found a sense of purpose and I felt freer of all expectations, my own and others. I now feel content with life.'

Now, as he prepared to approach what we understand as midlife, he felt hopeful, changed, and that he was finally living with purpose.

Midlife only became a concept in relatively recent history, with the dawn of gerontology in the 1960s, when improvements in healthcare in the developed world dramatically increased average life expectancy in the Western world into the late 60s and beyond. What would people do with this extra time afforded them? The lack of generativity and virility implied within the midlife crisis paradigm (as this was originally a predominantly male narrative) was directly linked to post-war, capitalist ideals of being useful, successful and having a certain standing in society. The view was that, post-retirement or approaching retirement, people were no longer active, contributing or participating. Worse for women, midlife was associated with no longer being biologically useful or attractive – at best reduced, at worst, utterly irrelevant.

It was in 1965 that Canadian psychoanalyst Elliott Jaques coined the now ubiquitous term 'midlife crisis' to describe the psychological conflict that he believed many people experience in the middle years of their lives, and this idea still holds currency today (Jackson, 2020). According to Jaques, this crisis is caused by a person's realisation that they are no longer young and that their death is approaching. This can lead to feelings of despair and loss and a reassessment of their life, prompting drastic changes in an attempt to find meaning and fulfilment (1965/1970). This construction arguably prevails today. Midlife in women is seen as being mostly synonymous with symptoms of menopause; midlife in men is personified with the idea of 'crisis'.

While the term is widely used and understood, as with any aspect of human experience, we must be careful with generalisations as they can isolate people and obfuscate their lived experience. When we therapists get alongside someone in their midlife, in whatever capacity, our best endeavour is to understand where they are at: crisis or growth, reduced or emboldened, relevant or irrelevant, excited or fearful, immune or overwhelmed, avoiding or engaging. All responses are unique and valid.

Let's get closer to the picture and see some of the wealth of details. The contemporary prevailing portrayal of midlife in the media is characterised by two competing narratives: crisis or renewal. On one hand, midlife is often depicted as being marked by feelings of anxiety, disillusionment and regret. The media frequently portray individuals in midlife as struggling with issues such as ageing, career dissatisfaction and relationship problems. People are often depicted as being in a state of transition, grappling with the realisation that their youth and opportunities are slipping away and that their lives have not turned out as they had hoped. This social and cultural construction can create a sense of fear or avoidance as this phase approaches. Populist depictions of the 'midlife crisis', Jaques' legacy, dominate even now, suggesting that individuals in their 40s and 50s may be so disillusioned with their lives that they feel compelled to make dramatic changes to regain a sense of purpose and meaning.

This notion is most often attributed to men, far less to women, but more on that later.

We can also see evidence of, and a growing movement for, midlife regeneration. As we shed the constraints of youth, we can embrace a new phase of life characterised by wisdom, freedom and creativity. Notions of conscious ageing have now made it out of academic papers and into social and broadcast media. The anti-ageism movement is powerful, driven by writers, journalists, gerontologists and some policy makers. For more on this, it is worth looking at the growing body of research and writing – the work of people such as Ashton Applewight, Tracey Gendron, Chip Conley, Avivah Wittenberg-Cox and Cindy Gallop in the US and Kathryn Collas and Fiona McKay in the UK. It is additionally powerful because the people driving it, mostly in their middle age, are part of what Saga (2023), a leading provider of products and services to the over-50s, calls 'Generation Experience'. Saga's research into the value that older adults bring to UK society found that this generation contributes £847 billion to the UK economy annually in monetary terms (2023). In the US, it is $8.3 trillion annually, or 40% of Gross Domestic Product, and is predicted to increase by 50% by 2030 (Accius & Joo Yeoun, 2019). This is due not only to income generation, spending and charitable giving but also to the significant burden of informal caring, volunteering and unpaid work that older generations contribute across most social and economic groups worldwide. Can we have it both ways? Is midlife a time when our power decays or it is a time when we are freed of the shackles and expectations of youth and more able to drive forward?

Developmental theorists rarely agree about the 'usual' trajectory of life changes. In his book on transition, writer and broadcaster Bruce Feiler (2021) passionately deconstructs the received idea of linear, predictable, phased development of self that was originated by the likes of Erik Erikson and Elliott Jaques and perpetuated by Daniel Levinson, Gail Sheehy and many others. And he is right: how can anyone speak to a universal experience? Individual, cultural, social and economic context will affect all our lived experiences.

A detailed study in 1996 into life transitions revealed that, while specific socially constructed age marker points exist, our life-course is nuanced, diverse and flexible. Our family context and rules, and the free will and proclivities of each individual, play an important part in determining how we experience our life trajectory (Settersten et al., 1996). Arguably, with the domination and immediacy of social media in contemporary life, the social and cultural influence on our life trajectory is more powerful. Conversely, the resulting rise and celebration of individualism through this same medium may also serve as just the boost we need to impel us to chart our own particular course.

The media's portrayal of midlife can have a significant impact on a person's experience of this life stage. In the counselling room, this is something we can actively explore to find clues to each client's lived experience and beliefs. Why are people drawn to one narrative or another? Jane, herself a major contributor to the economy and society, had always felt compelled to help others. In fact, it was one of the central building blocks of her identity, leading to her decision to adopt, her career choice, her caring roles with older parents and her various volunteer roles. Her parents had both been teachers, and in their retirement both became very active in their community. Her mother was a governor of a local school and her father a lay preacher in his church. Yet, through the course of our counselling sessions, as we explored the possibility (and even the necessity) of her retiring relatively early, she was beginning to discover that this unassuming but productive version of middle and later age was not necessarily for her.

As we began to work deeper into Jane's sense of confusion that day, she began to verbalise her thoughts. We had been meandering around some frequently recurring themes for some time. Today, however, quite unexpectedly, a torrent of ideas, judgements and stories began to flow, unfiltered. It felt for a moment as if I was inside her internal narrative, rather than in conversation with her.

'You see, I always thought I would retire and then spend most of my time reading, swimming when I feel able, doing yoga and seeing my friends. But I mean, then I really am the cliché, right? I mean, talk about self-indulgent! So, then I also always thought I'd need time to keep myself available to help the kids when they need it, and Lara [her daughter] needs such a lot from me at the moment, as you know, but who knows when the others might need support, or even have kids. Oh, my goodness, grandchildren?!' At this, she widened her eyes and momentarily looked lost in a tableau of her own making. 'And then I love the little bit of volunteering I do for a local charity, and then there is Dave's mum who needs a lot of our time each day really. So that should be enough, right? But now it is here, now I am here, at this point, I think, well… I think *God no!* Part of me wants all of that but I think that's just the future I planned for myself a long time ago. What would you counsellors call it…? A fantasy or something? Now it is here, I just find myself thinking of all the things I can do now, if I am well enough, obviously. Maybe I could become a coach? Or maybe I could become a lecturer in my specialism? Or I could buy some property and develop that. I could travel, alone if I could – Dave and I would not travel well together. I literally have no idea what might happen, but I think the buzzing I described is probably because of all of that.'

Her voice descended at the end of the sentence, and her hands, which had been orchestrating her words, returned to her lap, but this time upturned, as if asking a question. She stared at me. I stayed quiet for a little while, and she laughed loudly, breaking the silence: 'And now you are going to say, "That was a lot". Right?'

I smiled, co-conspiratorially. Over the course of the two years we had been meeting, Jane had got to know my tendencies well, and one of the artefacts of our sessions had been her trying to second-guess what I might say or how I might react. To keep us in the present and in our current process, I felt it was right to bring our focus back around to her lived experience in this moment. I asked, 'Well, did it feel like a lot when you expressed it?'

'No, it felt quite cathartic and helpful,' she replied.

'Your experience of letting that all out felt good.'

'Mmm,' she assented.

'Because?' I encouraged a little more to come.

'Well, because, I don't know, I think this has all been spinning around in my head, and sitting here and verbalising it gets it out and lets me sort through it a little more logically.'

'Yes, so now that it is out, I am wondering what you heard just then or where it leaves you.'

'I'm not so sure, really. The thing that I think I am left with most is surprise. Because of my illness and where I am in my career and life in general, I think of myself as having to slow down and consolidate, spend time helping others and giving back, but there is obviously a big part of me that wants more of a dramatic change.'

'And…?'

'And that's quite cool.' Jane paused, looked at me hard, and added, 'And quite scary'.

A counsellor's role is always to explore the unique lived reality of our client's world, listen out for clues, challenge constructs of their own or other's making, and encourage them, with us as their companion, to bravely face up to that which is painful or holding them back or in crisis. We simultaneously represent 'the other' – someone who experiences our client's way of being in the world – and, as Ernesto Spinelli calls it, 'the exception to the rule' (2006). We provide a different experience. I find the challenge of this quiet subversion very rewarding for me personally, in my role and for clients in general. We can broadly hold ideas and philosophies as a framework, but the only truth is the one being revealed, in all its potential, as the counselling process unfolds. Midlife is so rife with stereotypes that we must actively resist being seduced by them.

In this session, and others that followed, Jane and I began to explore where her need to help might have developed and how it served her (and didn't) in her life. Her early life had been quite transient, with some periods of living overseas. She remembered having repeatedly to find ways to fit in. Being compliant with and supporting others brought her instant regard from the people she was hoping would be her friends. Further to this, as the oldest of two, she remembers feeling that her younger sister was more wanted than her, or better than her, in some way.

'I was expected to get on with things and be quite independent from an early age and help show my sister the way. As I got a little older and we moved again, I was also expected to look after her. Neither of us had strong friendship groups due to moving about so much, and my parents usually both worked. My parents would say she was the bright one and I was the placid one, and I guess that sort of stuck with me.'

I was curious about her language here. 'You used the word "expected" a couple of times. Was this an explicit request or something you picked up and acted on, do you think?'

Jane shrugged, narrowed her eyes a little as if she wasn't understanding my question. 'Are you saying I made it up?'

'Ah no, not at all.'

I resisted the urge to immediately backtrack, as I felt a little ashamed by my clumsy expression, but it seemed to me that there was something revealing in Jane's instinctive response. 'How would it be for you if I was implying that?'

'I would be cross. In fact, I guess I am cross.'

'Can you say more?' I wanted to see what would come from this and felt it could hold some awareness for Jane that might be useful.

'Well, I spent a lot of my life doing things for others and maybe I lost time and should have been doing more for myself. Maybe that's behind this need for change now. And then you are kind of saying to me that I didn't need to, after all.'

I always get a tingling sensation when I am with a client and we come to what the textbooks call a 'rupture' – so-called with reference to Donald Winnicott's theory of the process of rupture and repair that is so central to the infant and caregiver relationship (1971). Attachment theory claims that this closely attuned attention from one to another is what allows us to develop a secure sense of self from which we can begin to explore the world. But the rockiness of ruptures along the road is often deeply uncomfortable. And I remember I had this tingling then. I see it as my body's way of preparing itself for an attack, but also there is also an awkwardness and an anticipation of a possibility of something new. It is a sign for me that we are about to move through it to a more attuned place in our relationship – one of deeper understanding. The process of the therapeutic encounter is, after all, one of living lives together, of bumping into each other, clumsily or otherwise, rather than solving problems (Spinelli, 2007); in Emmy van Deurzen's words, it is a 'collaborative, encouraging dialogue between two struggling human beings' (van Deurzen et al., 2019, p.3).

So, I stayed in the awkwardness. 'What is it like to be angry at me, or "cross", as you put it?'

'I just don't like it.' Jane gave another shrug and looked away.

'It's uncomfortable,' I said.

'Yes.'

'It is uncomfortable for me too; I feel like I missed you or didn't see you in what I said. And I feel guilty for that and, I suppose, a bit defensive.'

'Oh.'

'So, I think we are now both uncomfortable!'

Jane laughed and the tension was briefly diffused. We had shifted a little, but I didn't want to lose our thread. 'What made it uncomfortable for you?'

She gave a big sigh, and her shoulders relaxed a bit. 'I like to be liked, and it is also really important to me that I like you, I suppose.'

'And if being liked and liking people is important to you, it feels like that might also be something that naturally leads you to be a "helper" in some way?'

Jane nodded and her eyes flashed. 'Yes, I think it does, and it makes me cross with myself, now you say it that way.'

'I'm wondering if you are using "cross" as a substitute for another emotion, one that is less palatable or familiar to you.'

'Like anger?' Jane shot back.

'Well, does that fit?' I asked.

She nodded. 'I think it does, anger isn't something I feel I "do", but now I think about whether I have always lived my life trying to please people, I feel a bit angry. With myself, at least. And maybe with others too. Argh! I don't really know what to do with any of this. I am not an angry person!'

The social stereotype of women entering midlife and menopause is complex and multifaceted. It is often depicted as a time of physical and emotional upheaval, marked by symptoms such as hot flushes, mood swings and weight gain. Women going through menopause are generally expected to be irritable, forgetful, emotionally volatile and unable to cope with the challenges of daily life. Women are victims of, or are suffering with, this experience. Far more damaging are the cultural and social stereotypes of middle age that depict women as physically unattractive, barren, asexual, menopausal, depressed, irritable, frustrated and intellectually dulled (Degges-White & Myers, 2006). When female clients come to counselling at this stage of their lives, they may not yet be aware of the impact of this narrative on them, but it is worth listening out for it – just as it is worth listening out for, and seeking to understand, your own experience as a counsellor.

In my own counselling, as my perimenopause experience unfolded, I noticed how many times I was referencing my own anger. Things that never bothered me before began to provoke strong reactions in me. I felt a pull towards feminism, saw misogyny almost everywhere and despaired at the patriarchal society I felt I still lived in. I have found this anger connects me with a rich and vital seam of other women's experiences and gives me strength. In a frank account of her own menopause, journalist Caitlin Moran captures this internal shift, sardonically expressing a universal experience (2020):

> The menopause has stopped her being so blithe and forgiving. It's uncovered her actual personality and thoughts, underneath all the hormones. This is a very important distinction… If an older woman gets angry, people often react as if there's something temporarily wrong with her… rather than realising the truth, that this is who she is now.

The experience of anger has been new to me. Throughout my life, I have felt awkward about, even ashamed of acknowledging anger. I grew up in a household with a father who was quick to express anger, which he did vocally and viscerally, and just as quick to move beyond it once it was aired, and a mother who herself grew up in a family where relationships might be described as diplomatic at best and considerately avoidant at worst. She often minimised the impact of my father's anger when it appeared. This was kind, but also confusing, and I think this explains my ambivalence about it. Now, as I move into menopause, my anger has grown, and I feel it giving me a gathering strength. But, knowing that 'the angry woman' is one of the archetypes of midlife, this has occasionally made me uncomfortable too.

My therapist helped me move beyond this, very simply, and probably in a way that she wouldn't even remember. When reflecting something back at me one day, she said, 'I can hear you are very angry about that, Helen,' to which I flashed back, 'I am not angry. I am, in fact, well, rageful.' 'Aaaah, so it is rage,' she replied, with a hint of complicity, but with no prejudgement or assumptions about why; 'And that distinction feels important'. This straightforward affirmation of my lived experience without stereotypical framing felt powerfully important. The word 'rage' fitted snugly into my experience, and from then I felt a little taller and more righteous. Never have I felt more seen in a counselling session.

Jane was one of the most forthright yet understated people I have met. As we explored how she experienced anger, she frequently said she found it difficult. I wanted to challenge this, or at least find some depth in it, as it felt important at this pivotal time when she was considering who she was. 'I'm struck,' I told her, 'by how uncomfortable with anger you say you feel and yet I remember so many times when you have described standing up for yourself, or for others, when you felt it was important. And how passionately you do this. I am wondering how this is different to anger?'

Jane pondered, her foot circling slowly in one direction and then another. This was a familiar characteristic, usually signifying discomfort for her or entering new territory. I circled mine a little in echo and asked, 'What's happening with your foot?' 'I don't know,' she replied. 'Something I don't want to admit maybe, something I am avoiding?'

'Do you have a hunch?' I asked.

'I think it's because you are right in some way, but I'm not ready to see it.'

'You don't feel ready to make that connection.'

'Yep.'

'Tell me about standing up for yourself. When did it last happen?'

'Well, at work with that colleague of mine I told you about who always seems to belittle me or criticise me. Just yesterday, she questioned my approach to something, in front of our team – something she knows very little about, in fact. I was indignant, but I called it out on the spot, explained my point of view and exposed her lack of knowledge at the same time.'

'And that felt…?' I encouraged her to find more connection.

'Easy, good, powerful, I suppose.' Jane pondered.

'And you said "indignant", so is this another word for angry, really?'

'Yes.'

'But this didn't make you uncomfortable, it made you feel powerful.'

'Yes!'

'Let's see if we can understand why…' I started, but Jane interrupted.

'Aha, I know why, actually. I am on firm ground at work. I am sure of my role, and I am sure of myself. There are clear rules, and I am good at it. I am in control.' She punctuated all this by punching her fist into her other palm.

'Does anger perhaps make you feel out of control?'

'Yes, maybe, but only in life, in relationships and all of that messy stuff.'

I began to feel that some of the early relational dynamics in Jane's life might have caused her to feel she always had to be compliant, helpful, easy to engage with. This way, there was harmony and she had very successfully developed it into a way of being that worked well for her in her early career and motherhood. What we had been exploring here was how easy it was for her to tolerate anger towards others and still hold a cohesive sense of herself as helpful and accommodating. When we had tested that in our moment of misattunement, she wasn't comfortable with it. However, work was a different matter; here, the rules were clear, and she felt she was allowed to be strong in her opinions and to advocate for herself.

In our sessions after this, Jane oscillated between feeling restless and excited about the future and frustrated with her life in the here and now – with the relapses and limitations of her health, dynamics within her family and her relationship with her husband. In some ways, we progressed steadily in ever-decreasing circles, following the threads of these themes and gaining more clarity but also more urgency about what Jane wanted next in her life. Sometimes in counselling we don't have big, pivotal moments where everything becomes clear. They happen very infrequently, in fact. But I believe what happens instead is a continual unfurling of self, so that what is revealed is almost already there and known when it finally gains form. Being witness to that as it happens is a huge privilege.

With Jane, this moment – one of them at least – came relatively undramatically. She had been reducing her workload to cope with illness and was feeling more energised and also clearer headed as a result. 'One of the things I keep thinking about,' she announced one day, almost out of the blue, 'is that I have very little energy to go round but I seem to give all of it to other people.'

'Can you say more?' I encouraged.

'Well, that all seems a little ridiculous, doesn't it?'

I nodded.

'My children will always get my energy, but I think I am done with giving it out when I get nothing back.'

'You are done.'

'Yes, it's like you said ages ago, people have these expectations of me, and I probably don't ever stop to say no, or "This doesn't work for me", so I am part of the problem really. But if I stopped to think for a minute, I might have a different response.'

'Like…?'

'Like, "Do it your bloody self!" Or "Find someone else to help." Or "I can do it but not right now." Because the thing is, I really feel this time needs to be more about me. And if people don't like that, then…' She trailed off.

'Then…?'

'Well, they will have to live with it. I mean I have always wanted to go back to uni, do other qualifications or retrain. My kids are grown up, I am financially stable so I really can do that now. Can't I?'

I laughed. 'Are you asking for my permission, or is that rhetorical?'

'Nah, I don't need it. I *can* do that now, I know that.' And she sighed again. Only this was not a sigh of defeat; it was almost jubilant.

Something huge within Jane was shifting, but established patterns and ways of being were holding her back from moving into a new and exciting space. Cultural expectations about how she should be as a woman nearing 60, as well as her own, life-long expectations of 'acceptable' behaviour, were blocking her attempts to discover how she really wanted to be in this new phase. My role – and privilege – as her counsellor was to be aware of these established narratives and stereotypes, to collaborate and be curious with her, and to provide a non-judgemental space for these emergent experiences to surface and be explored.

Chapter 2
Working well

Around the world women continue to be disadvantaged by a working culture that is based on the ideological belief that male needs are universal.
Caroline Criado Perez, *Invisible Women* (2020, p.19)

All the world's a stage, and all the men and women merely players. They have their exits and their entrances; And one man in his time plays many parts.
William Shakespeare, *As You Like It* (1623/1993, p.185)

'I don't mind telling you, I am really very good at my job, and I love it.'

Donna was a successful sales executive. She had been in the same job with the same company for 25 years and had been counting down the years until retirement. The prospect of the generous pension guaranteed at the end of her career would be the ultimate pay-off and provide welcome security in her retirement years. She had moved to the UK from her home in Zimbabwe to study and then to work. Her daughter had been born not long afterwards. The father of her child was supportive but was never destined to be Donna's life partner. When she came to counselling, she was single, had been single for most of her (now adult) daughter's life, and her career had been central not only to her independence but also to her identity. But in the months leading up to her coming to counselling, her job had started to become toxic. Anxieties and self-doubt were creeping in, fuelled by awful insomnia and crippling headaches, resulting in a dip in her performance, and now poor treatment by her managers. In our first session, she told me of the crushing lack of confidence she was experiencing and a strong sense of not knowing who she was anymore. She felt like a failure. If she couldn't stay in her job, who might she be? What would she do?

'I don't mind telling you, I am really very good at my job, and I love it.' She said the words triumphantly and with a decisive nod of the head. We had been talking about identity, in relation to a man she had been dating over the previous month or so. She'd noticed he had a habit of dismissing her work, and she'd wondered if he was threatened by it. I admit that I had found myself veering between total awe of her and mild intimidation by her poise and confidence. She was always dressed neatly and colourfully. Her dark hair always perfectly framed her face and her nails were always impeccable. I didn't doubt for a second that she was good at her job. I was curious about why she felt she needed to preface the statement with 'I don't mind', but we would get to that later.

In 2022, BUPA published a survey revealing that an estimated one million women in the UK have left their job because of the menopause (BUPA, 2022). This statistic contributed enormously to the growing concern in recent years about the impact of menopause not only on women's lives but also on the productivity of our workforce and national economy as a whole. In the UK, more than 72% of women are in paid employment (Francis-Devine & Hutton, 2024), and they make up nearly half of the UK workforce (Kopenhager & Guidozzi, 2015). Women are also now working for longer than they did in the past. The biggest increase in employment rates over the past 30 years have been among women aged 60–64 (from 18% to 41%) and 55–59 (from 49% to 69%) (Women & Equalities Committee, 2022). Strikingly, women occupy 77% of the jobs in the health and social work sector and 70% in education. Throughout and since the Covid pandemic, women have been on the frontline, ensuring that people receive the health and care they need and our children continue to receive an education (Women & Equalities Committee, 2022; Francis-Devine & Hutton, 2024). The significance of these data is clear: supporting women to thrive through midlife at work is not only important to each of these individuals but also vital to our economy. In her foreword to a 2022 government consultation call on women's health, the then Minister for Health and Social Care Nadine Dorries concluded the same:

> Investing in all aspects of women's health, including within the workplace, is essential to women's ability to reach their full potential and contribute to the communities in which they live. (UK Government, 2022)

However, without credible counter-arguments, the statistics showing women leaving work during menopause will dominate the narrative and, unwittingly, create the impression that women are simply unable to cope. It is important to balance this narrative and leave room also for the possibility that women may be leaving work because they see midlife as a time to reconsider their career choices. I think it is important for practitioners and workplaces to support the wellbeing, growth and agency of women who are navigating their daily lives and careers through the maelstrom of midlife, so that they are empowered and not reduced. The poet-philosopher David Whyte observes (1994, p.231), 'Human beings find it necessary to sacrifice their own sacred desires and personal visions at the altar of work and success'. Life transitions are indeed times when we can reacquaint ourselves with our own self, and they can also be a time when we discover what our true desires are and have the courage, or freedom, to pursue them.

As counsellors, we hold space for many things in our conversations with clients – for darkness, pain, fear and confusion. But we are also the harbingers of possibility and potentiality, even when the people we work with are not yet in a place to recognise them. Slowly and carefully, while witnessing the many stories that need to come forth, we lay down fertile soil for growth. We believe growth is possible, even, and especially, when clients are not yet ready to believe it.

A study, some years old now, into transitions and counselling with midlife women, concluded that 'midlife is a time of activity and movement, rather than a period of inactivity and stagnation,' and that the women who participated in the research reported 'living lives full of activity and expansion' (Degges-White & Myers, 2006, p.147). In my own research for this book, I met many women who reported the same. Lisa, 50, told me that, despite experiencing menopausal symptoms through her late 40s, she wasn't afraid of ageing. She was mother to two grown-up children, whose leaving the family home had given her a renewed feeling of freedom. Having reached a good point in her career as a management accountant, she felt a pull towards doing more meaningful work. She had approached her workplace initially to talk about how she could adapt her role to cope with her menopause symptoms, which were mostly disrupted sleep and cognition and memory problems. She had been leading an important client account and wanted to make sure she had support in place to still succeed in this while working through her physical symptoms and changes. These conversations, and talking to friends and family, had led her to consider whether she wanted something different. Twelve months into those conversations, she left her job to take a career break, and embarked on a university course in sustainability. She told me: 'It's such an exciting and new phase of life and this new direction undoubtedly started with the menopause. I'm not sure exactly where it will take me, but I feel like what I am doing is meaningful.'

Lisa acknowledged that having a job with purpose and personal meaning for her was something she had possibly always wanted but she hadn't found a way to do that until now.

Returning to the counselling room and Donna, I acknowledged what she had said about her job, but added, 'There feels to be something more in that statement. I'm not sure what, but it feels important in some way.'

'How do you mean?' Donna asked.

I spread my hands and reminded her, 'You said, "I don't mind telling you" at the start.'

Donna looked to one side, considering this carefully: 'Ah yes I did.' She paused before continuing, 'I think my career, my job rather, defines me, in terms of how people think of me I mean, but sometimes not in a good way.'

I wasn't sure I completely understood, so I waited to see what else came.

'Yeah,' she said, more definitely now, 'I think I come across as kind of successful but, because I don't have a husband or a big family or anything else in my life, apart from Darcy [her daughter], I suppose

I often feel people don't see the real me, or make certain assumptions about me. That they think that's all I am, and it's a bit dull.'

'And how is that for you? What comes up as you say that to me?' I asked.

'I feel frustrated, and I think with this new man I am seeing, I think he probably does that. It makes me defensive.'

We had only been working together for a few weeks at this point. It occurred to me that I regarded Donna in these initial weeks largely through the lens of her capability and poise. As this particular session progressed, I shared this with her, using how we related in the counselling room as a mirror of her relationships with others in the rest of her life. Next, I invited her to consider how she responded to my sharing that I sometimes felt in awe of her composure and confidence. 'I like it!' she laughed.

'I guess we can be curious about that,' I continued. 'What does it give you when people respond in that way?'

'It gives me confidence and, at work, it gives me power, in a way. Even on my worst of days, people won't know that I am feeling wobbly.'

'So, in a way it is a form of defence?'

'Yes, I think it is definitely that.'

'It makes me curious about what you are defending.'

'Erm, probably weakness. No – definitely weakness.' We both let these words settle a little.

'Just now, you said you felt that people only saw you in one way, and it frustrated you,' I said.

'Yes?' She didn't seem sure of what I was saying yet, so I continued. 'Do you think in anyway the confident exterior also takes something from you as well as giving you something?'

'Like?'

'Like maybe a connection or realness?'

'Hmmm.' Donna was considering this but replied, 'I don't know what you mean.'

I suggested we try something, and asked Donna's permission to do so.

'Can you sit inside yourself for a minute? I know that sounds silly but really just imagine yourself climbing down inside your body and being fully inside it and present.'

'Okay...' she closed her eyes for a few seconds and settled a little in her chair, breathing in. 'Yes. I'm there.'

'Can you describe for me who you are today, here, right in this moment?'

'Erm, right. Well, I am a bit distracted today. I am coming here in my lunchtime, and there is a big report to get finished so I am not completely here, my head is a bit fuzzy.'

'Okay, your head is fuzzy and a bit distracted.'

'Yes.'

'What else? Keep focusing inwards if you can.'

'Well, I feel a bit mushy. These new HRT drugs I am on make me feel bloated and like I am putting on weight and my body doesn't feel so nice.'

'So, your body feels a bit mushy.'

We went on in this way, Donna noticing parts of her experience and me affirming them. When we were finished, she looked at me questioningly. I asked how she had found it and she said she hadn't realised how much was going on inside her until she sat and thought about it. I am sure Donna knew where I was going next; it wasn't intended to be clever, just thought-provoking.

'And yet, from the outside what I am experiencing is that you are very calm, collected and focused.'

At this, Donna laughed. 'Yep, trademark me!'

'But it's not the whole story. When I was repeating back to you how you were feeling – fuzzy, mushy and so on – how was that?'

'Honestly, it was a bit weird,' she said, and we both laughed, 'but it does make me realise that, if I only project one thing, people will only think of me in one way.'

These moments, when we come to a client encounter with an idea of what might be helpful, are a powerful lesson for me in how to simply hold the space and trust that we could start a little fire that takes a while to burn. Had anything therapeutic happened here? I couldn't know. I had hoped to provide Donna with the experience of feeling, within our microcosmic bubble, that someone was attuned to, or really tuned into, who she was in that moment. In existential therapy, it is said that therapists offer clients both a representative of others in the world and an alternative possibility to how they experience themselves (Spinelli, 2006). I wanted to give Donna a safe experience of showing all of the messiness of her lived experience and it being accepted. It's not so different from the way humans communicate with the very young. Watch any parent or adult interact with a small child: we go down to their level, play with them, mimic their gestures and noises back at them and encourage them to be messy and creative. What they receive is validation and reassurance of their place and safety in the world at a time when they are still inherently vulnerable and unsure of who they are. The way we hold people within a therapeutic setting is not so different.

Donna continued to struggle at work, and this became the focus of many of our conversations. She told me how she was second-guessing herself in a way she had never done. Instinct and charm had carried her easily before; now everything felt harder. She was nervous before client meetings and stumbled over sales pitches that she had given a hundred times before. This was exacerbated by her boss relentlessly raising expectations and communicating her disappointment at Donna's lack of progress. Donna had begun to describe a growing anxiety and feeling of overwhelm, which was also negatively impacting her sleep. I received an email out of the blue one Monday morning, asking if we could move our Friday session to earlier in the week. I had time available the following morning, and Donna confirmed she would like to take it.

Donna was visibly upset when she arrived at my door the next day. Gone were the usual formal work clothes, now replaced by sportswear and trainers, and she wore no make-up. I gently ushered her into my room. She reached for a handful of tissues as she sat down and, through her tears, told me that she had been called into a meeting the previous day and been told she was at risk of redundancy. Seemingly, in her small team of colleagues, she was the only one at risk. 'I am so glad I could come here and let this all out. I was crying at work yesterday and I just didn't want people seeing me like that. Nobody needs me to lose my shit. I mean, my own team need me to be strong, don't they?'

I didn't answer, sensing this was not a direct question, but I nodded, encouraging her to continue.

'And you are going to tell me that I don't have to be strong, I can show people my feelings, but I don't feel I want to yet. I don't even know what they are!'

'I wonder if we can spend some time today working that out, if that's helpful?'

'I don't know how to do that!' Donna ran her hand across her face and covered her eyes as she said it.

Writing in *The Guardian*, journalist and menopause podcaster Lorraine Candy eloquently captured the experience of 'an army' of women, gleaned from her own research, for whom midlife had taken away their ability to deal with life stressors almost overnight (2023). She went on to explain that this is caused in part by our body's changing hormone levels in our mid-40s to mid-50s, but also acknowledged that our changing identity may cause us to rethink how we want to live our life. Seen from an existential viewpoint, as expressed by existential philosopher Martin Heidegger and others, our experience of overwhelm, or anxiety, is a privilege. It is precisely our anxiety that allows us to be confronted fully with the responsibilities and dilemmas of living; it is educative, and it carries us towards our true, authentic self. It frames our fears within our own experience (Kirkland-Handley & Mitchell, 2005). Existential theory encourages therapists to welcome anxiety and work creatively with it to reveal greater insights for our clients into how they want to live their lives (Cooper, 2003). I had a growing sense that there was a shift within Donna, maybe very deep and not yet acknowledged, that was bringing about her change in demeanour towards work, and that her anxiety might be trying to reveal something that would ultimately move her forward. I didn't want to get ahead of myself, so I stayed with what was happening for Donna, reminding myself to closely attune to what she was saying and how she was expressing it and to my own resonances.

'Well, there isn't "a way" of doing this,' I reassured Donna. 'Let's talk and see what comes out and where it takes us.'

What came out, in a long and many-branched account, was less important than where it got us to. For context and completeness, it is worth noting that Donna felt that her anxiety and lowering confidence, while she didn't admit them to anyone at work, had got in the way of her making some of the big sales she would usually make. Her sales figures had dropped, even if only a little, and this made her more anxious. She hadn't spoken to anyone about this directly. Her new boss had heard great things about Donna and had come in with high expectations, which weren't being met. Donna felt angry, misunderstood and, she said, ashamed.

'Ashamed?'

'I'm a salesperson. Our job is to be confident. To be compelling. To not be able to do that is just embarrassing. I mean, who am I if I can't even do that?'

I raised an eyebrow.

She sighed. 'I know, I know, I am much more than that etc etc. But it is important to me…'

Donna was referring to our previous sessions where we had been exploring all the different parts of her identity, and the time in the early sessions when we had contrasted her outward confidence with her inner landscape. I could feel her frustration; she seemed to be saying that she needed to grieve this part of herself first, that she didn't want me to invite all the other parts forward. This dissonance between varying parts of people's self creates powerful opportunities in therapy. Through becoming fluent and accomplished in having this plurality, people can live fully and freely in the way they choose (Mearns & Thorne, 2000). However, this takes time and I wanted to respect the feelings Donna had just expressed.

I paused, 'I am so sorry this is happening for you. I can feel with you how complex and upsetting it is.' Donna nodded.

I went on. 'I am hearing a lot about what people are saying, what the numbers are saying and what is needed of you. I wonder if we can get into what you are experiencing.' I involuntarily touched my own hand to my chest while I explained to Donna that I hoped we could gain a closer connection to what she instinctively wanted and needed by exploring her lived experience, rather than only the facts and details.

'Can you put yourself back in one of those selling situations, for a moment. What was happening for you?'

'I can think of the last one, a few weeks ago. I was fully prepared; it was someone I knew quite well. I felt fairly relaxed going in, I suppose. As I started to go through the presentation, something changed, I don't really know what, and I lost the thread and it all went wrong. I think they could tell that I lost my conviction.'

'Something changed?'

'Yes, like something inside me, I think.'

'As you recall it now do you get a sense of it?'

'Erm… not really.'

'Colour, shape, noise, words?' I encouraged.

Donna sighed. 'I don't really know. I suppose the word that comes to me, weirdly, is that I was bored. That sounds strange because I know I was feeling worried. But as you said that just then, I could only hear the word "bored".'

'Bored.'

'Yes.'

'Does it feel right? If you go back into that memory, does "bored" feel right?'

'Actually, yes.'

'Aha.'

'I think on that day, and now I think of it, on other days too, I could feel myself run out of steam. Like I couldn't be bothered suddenly. Like it didn't mean as much to me.'

'I'm curious about what "it" is,' I said, mainly because I wanted to make sure I stayed with her but also to try and help Donna focus in on this experience.

'Ah, yes. Erm, I suppose I meant "the win". But as I am saying it, I think I also mean, maybe, the job itself.' Here, Donna's eyes widened in surprise. 'Oooh, where did that come from?'

'That surprises you,' I smiled.

'Yes.' She paused. 'I have always had this sort of north star, which is the goal that I will stay doing this and enjoying it, and at the end of it I will get my big retirement cheque and that is all I need.'

'And…?'

'Well, I am just thinking now, what if that isn't what I want?'

A recent report on *Women in the Workplace*, based on a survey of 22,000 women and 18,000 men (Field et al., 2023), found that it was increasingly important to women that they work for companies that prioritise career development, flexibility, wellbeing and diversity, equality and inclusion. 'Women are demanding more from work, and they're leaving their companies in unprecedented numbers to get it,' the report concluded. I think it is worth remembering this context and balancing it with the data around women leaving the workforce due to menopausal (or any other physical or psychological) factors. Midlife is a huge transition, and it is exactly that – a change from something into something else that is new. To add to this, many women I spoke to, and some of the emerging social narratives, are moving away from constructing midlife as encompassing only menopause. The management accountant, Lisa, was angry about this when I spoke with her. She told me, 'Not everything for women has to be about the menopause. We've gone from everything being about the period to everything being about the menopause!'

Others I spoke to agreed. Soraya, a PR consultant in her early 50s, rolled her eyes when I asked about her experience of menopause. She told me she was naturally an optimistic person who shrugged off bad things. 'I am a very determined and focused person, so when my menopause transition began, I read a lot and talked to others and made some adaptations, but I have a general sense of wellbeing, I feel at peace with myself. I don't want to be defined by this,' she said.

Soraya went on to tell me her view that, in India, where she grew up, there is naturally more resilience to physical symptoms, due to a legacy of hardship and an underfunded healthcare system that can't be relied on to support people in the same way as in Western societies. 'To a degree, I feel people in Western society have lost a thick skin. We are always expecting solutions to our health problems, but life can't be "won", as it were, and challenge is part of what it means to be alive.' She went on to explain that her menopause transition prompted her to leave the organisation she was with and set up her own business with a friend. She described how they were respectful of each other's space, and it felt good to be in control of her destiny. She told me there were days when she felt the fear of insecurity, but she liked that it had made her in some ways fearless, less cushioned and more courageous.

Fiona McKay is an advisor, researcher, influencer and speaker and the founder of The Menopause Maze, a support programme for professional women through menopause (https://www.themenopausemaze.com). She coaches women to keep their careers as they move through menopause and is known in the media as 'the Menopause Career Coach'. I was keen to talk to her and ask what advice she would give to those around and supporting people in their midlife transition. She told me: 'Midlife is a time of many questions. Don't feel you have to help people answer them all. At work we need to equip managers to think about each person in context. Work isn't transactional anymore – it is much more intimate. Help people get to know themselves and what they want from work.'

Fiona went on to say that we have a tendency to devalue midlife in our workplaces, whether they are male or female: 'People's currency devalues as we age, and we have to try to change that, by raising awareness. We have to be careful not to weaponise it but work as individuals to carve a path through it.'

But we need to balance the growth narrative with some of the realities of what it is like for women working through midlife and menopause. Undoubtedly there are many women whose menopausal symptoms are so present that they are completely unable to function in the same way they have before. The *Menopause and the Workplace* report, produced by the Fawcett Society and Channel 4, polled 4,000 women aged 45–55 and found that 10% had left their job due solely to symptoms of the menopause (Fawcett Society, 2022). Research shows that conditions related to women's health, such as heavy menstrual bleeding, endometriosis, pregnancy-related issues and the menopause, can affect women's workforce attendance, productivity and career outcomes. Women are more likely than men to have a long-term sickness absence and end up leaving work (UK Government, 2022). In a survey of more than 1,000 women on the impact of perimenopause and menopause at work (Balance, 2021), 99% said their perimenopausal or menopausal symptoms had negatively impacted their careers, 59% had taken time off as a result of their symptoms and half (50%) of those who took at least eight weeks off work subsequently resigned or took early retirement. And even if women can work, the burden of caregiving for children and elderly parents, as well as doing the housework, generally falls on women (UK Government, 2022). Being encumbered by all of that, alongside their job, at a time of physical and emotional vulnerability, is not sustainable for many women.

Irene, a project manager in the full swing of her menopause, told me: 'I struggle to remember simple things, sometimes even people's names. I have to write everything down. And even when I do remember, I doubt myself. Diligence and organisation are the most important parts of my job, and of my personality. It is incredibly humiliating, and I feel like I am failing. I can see my immediate boss watching me and wondering what is wrong with me and I don't know if I can carry on this way.'

Another woman I spoke to was paralysed by her symptoms to the point that she felt suicidal. 'It started with sleep problems when

I was around 45. I'd be awake and catastrophising at all hours, then I had crippling anxiety. I was so tired I couldn't exercise, and then I was bloating and putting on weight. I was having headaches daily. I couldn't engage with my work or my family and even if I wanted to have sex with my husband, it was too painful, so we stopped trying. My periods were heavy, sometimes I couldn't get out of bed, and I had these weird pins and needles all the time. Everywhere I turned, things were bad. I just couldn't see a way out.'

As she was telling me this, she seemed calm, detached and composed, which I mentioned to her. She said she was feeling mostly better now, but that it took nearly six months of this before she realised what was happening could be the menopause and she found a very understanding doctor who prescribed HRT and respected her preferences when she vehemently refused antidepressants.

Many women undoubtedly face unprecedented challenges at work within this midlife period. As women make up half of the workforce and, in the UK at least, middle-aged women are the fastest growing section of the workforce, supporting women to thrive through this time is not just kind, it is vital. By ignoring or not addressing the menopause, organisations may cause great distress; it needs to be acknowledged formally in workplaces and in our practice with clients (Griffiths et al., 2016).

Donna wasn't symptomatic at work in a way that she recognised, but she found work easier once she had started on HRT, as it helped with her disrupted sleep patterns and her memory. Our discussions had revealed something that had shifted. Throughout my training and in my counselling practice, I have been drawn to an existential humanistic outlook. I think this is mainly because of its philosophical foundations – I love the messy, imprecise humanness this philosophy has at its heart. I am also drawn to existentialism as it holds in equal balance the belief that we humans will suffer through living, but we also intrinsically have the potential for fierce self-knowledge and growth. It is neither pessimistic nor optimistic; it is simply realistic, and it is forward-moving. Its viewpoint is that we can all grow as individuals, given the right conditions and despite the dilemmas of life, but it also warns us that being inauthentic (not living how we want to) is sometimes unavoidable and can be seductive. Yet living inauthentically alienates us from ourselves eventually (van Deurzen et al., 2019; Cooper, 2003).

What I have valued in my personal therapy journey is the use of curiosity, creativity and active enquiry to find a way to be the expert and then the author of my experience and growth. This is the process I also aim to achieve with clients. Noticing what is happening and having a dialogue about why and how it happens helps us get a clear picture of our unique world, not just the world we fit into around others. The most important role and purpose of therapy is not to help; it is to facilitate the client to experience what is really happening and ask why (Mearns & Thorne, 2000). In this last session, Donna had stumbled across a new idea, one that she hadn't known was forming – that she might not be enjoying her job any more or want to follow the path on which she had resolutely set herself.

I stayed silent while Donna sat for a few moments with the idea that her job was no longer what she wanted. Then I reflected back to her: 'That felt like quite a big statement as you said it, but I also felt something about it sort of settled into you.'

I had sensed a relaxing of her body and of mine – a surrender maybe, as she had said it, but I wanted to know how it had been for her.

'Yeah, it was like when the words came out, they had been there all along I suppose, like it wasn't new to me.' She laughed. 'Sorry, that doesn't make much sense!'

'Does it make sense to you?' I asked.

She paused, 'Yes, strangely, it does.'

'How is your body responding to this?' I asked her.

'I feel relaxed for the first time since I got the call from HR – like stable and solid. I mean, my heart is kind of racing at the thought that I might want to change my job because honestly how is that practical or even doable at my age? It's crazy.' Her hands flew to her head in panic, and she paused. 'But, strange as it is to think it, I feel like it releases me from all the expectations, the rules I have to follow, the pushing of myself, even on bad days and when I feel uncertain about stuff. And if it is my choice, after all, then it feels just better as a story.' She said this emphatically and louder than the rest, her eyes wide. 'Yes, for everyone else, of course, but for myself too.'

When it feels like something important might be happening within a therapy session, I find it hard not to run away with my own views of where it might go and what it might be like for the other person. I think this is probably common among therapists. I try to hold the idea that, even when one part of a person wants to grow and change, there is a 'not-for-growth' part that may want us to wait or hold back. Person-centred approaches to therapy encourage counsellors to let all of these parts be heard and accepted (Mearns & Thorne, 2000), and existential approaches encourage a vibrant debate between them, with the therapist representing the 'they', the rest of the world, in a social nexus that allows meaning to emerge.

'And the story is…?' I encouraged.

'That I want more from my job. I haven't felt settled for a while. I want to do something different.'

'And how does it feel to say that out loud?' I challenged her.

'Argh. I'm terrified. I honestly think I might get out of here, walk into work and start fighting for my job, negotiating performance improvement, proving to them that I am better than they think, almost without realising it… Oh no, now you probably are disappointed,' she threw out quickly at the end.

I took this in. 'Donna, I think you have uncovered some new insight here today but none of it has to be "the truth", as it were. What we are in the business of doing is discovering more about yourself and your experience so you can find your way forward, through this, from a place of awareness and knowledge that you have choices. What you do is up to you. I am invested in you living in a way that feels right for you.'

Sometimes we say things for the client to ground them, educate them or help them pace themselves through the sessions. And sometimes we say things to ground both of us, educate both of us and keep us both on the path that is right for our client, and it resonates loudly. This was one of those occasions for me. What Donna chose to do was not important here; what was important was that she felt more connected to what was happening for her.

Not long into setting up my counselling practice, I went to a talk given by the existential psychotherapist and theorist Ernesto Spinelli. His books (2006, 2007) had nourished and inspired me during my training. Some way into the talk, he humbled the audience by telling us not to get too caught up on feeling as if something therapeutic was happening. 'I can't remember a single therapeutic act,' he told us. I remember thinking hard then about what it was all for. What is this strange business of therapy, of accompanying people through difficult, confusing and changing times? My conclusion, borne out by several more years of practice, is that we hold an idea for clients. The idea is hope, but it is more than that; it is the knowledge that something new will come from the process that is unique to the client and will take them somewhere. It will support them in transcending the narratives that they are caught within, or ideas and assumptions that have held them back, or societal and cultural structures and expectations that box them in.

Donna was in a job that, on the surface, was working well for her. As she approached midlife and things started to change at work, she could have chosen to feel she was a victim of her circumstances and to make that her narrative: that menopause, her life stage, had stolen her confidence and her employer had failed to support her. What we discovered, instead, was a part of her that had been ignored until now, that was pulling away and wanting something different. For Donna, this was terrifying, but it also released her to create a new story, one that was authentic to how she actually felt. Our work ended shortly after this, when the Covid pandemic hit and Donna decided not to transition to online sessions. She said she would be happy to take a break, and she didn't return, apart from a brief phone call two years later.

Statistics aside, there are numerous different stories of women's experiences of menopause in the workplace. Every woman will navigate it differently. The MP Caroline Nokes, Chair of the cross-party Women and Equalities Committee, passionately stated the following when she launched the 2022 UK Parliament report on menopause and the workplace:

> Menopause is inevitable. The steady haemorrhage of talented women from our workforce, however, is not. Stigma, shame and dismissive cultures can, and must, be dismantled. It is imperative that we build workplaces – and a society – which not only supports those going through the menopause but encourages some of the most experienced and skilled workers in our economy to thrive. (UK Parliament, 2022)

The last word of this statement is the one that stands out for me – 'thrive'. We therapists create a space where clients can move through their circumstances, become the authors of a new narrative, and thrive, wherever it takes them. I rather like this idea, particularly as we ride the wave of these major life transitions. One of my research interviewees summed it up perfectly: 'Menopause makes you feel that the world is closing in and being made smaller. I made a conscious, concerted effort to make my world bigger in response.'

Chapter 3
Strange bodies

We are not less of ourselves on the other side of this, we are more.
Heather Corinna, *What fresh hell is this? Perimenopause,*
menopause, other indignities, and you. (2021, p.19)

I think transwomen, and transpeople in general, show everyone
that you can define what it means to be a man or woman on your
own terms. A lot of what feminism is about is moving outside of
roles and moving outside of expectations of who and what you're
supposed to be to live a more authentic life.
Laverne Cox, *Here we are: Feminism for the real word.* (2017, p.75)

Folded in on herself in the counselling chair, Joanna was screwing her
face up in acute discomfort, unable to meet my gaze. We had been
talking about her experience of sex and we had hit the threshold of
her embarrassment. In her early 50s, slight, lithe and quietly spoken,
with a tangle of greying blonde hair piled on her head and a face that
spoke of an inquiring mind, Joanna had originally sought counselling
due to the ill health of both her parents. However, the process of self-
reflection had also exposed pressures in other aspects of her life, such
as her marriage. She and her husband had a mutual respect and a
shared history that had meant they had been mildly contented for
most of their 24 years together, if not happy, and inhabited very
traditional 'man-and-wife' roles.

Joanna had been telling me about an upcoming visit to see some friends, which meant an overnight hotel stay near to them, '… and this normally means we have to have sex, of course', she finished.

'Why "Of course"?' I asked; it felt automatic and perhaps sarcastic.

'Well, it's always this thing we have to do if we stay in a hotel, and, honestly, I can't be bothered to have the conversation with him about how I don't want to. It's easier just to do it.'

I nodded and let this sit between us for a moment.

Joanna cocked her head. 'What?'

'I guess I am wondering if this is how you want it to be this time?' I replied.

'It is just how it is!' said Joanna with a sigh. 'It's how it always is.'

Joanna and I had been working together for only a few months, but she understood the process of counselling. As operations director for a small charity, the counselling service it provided was one of the areas under her diligent, watchful eye. And yet, when it came to her own process and the flow of our dynamic in the room together, she was unconfident and guarded.

'So, I am left wondering what it would look like if you could change it?' I went on. 'If it wasn't just "How it always is".'

'Err… I think I would be in the hotel room with someone else! Crikey, I feel awful saying that.' She folded her arms now. 'But lately I have been feeling more of a… well, I suppose it's an urge… to try something new. Maybe.' Here she scrunched her face and winced.

'And I can see you have folded your arms and made a face. It feels like this is uncomfortable to say,' I noted gently. Joanna nodded.

'Why, I wonder?' I asked.

'I've just never thought about myself having needs or being a terribly sexual person. It's not a normal feeling for me,' she replied.

Who are women when their bodies shed their natural ability to reproduce and bear children? Who are men when their natural virility and fertility has waned? As the potency of the sexually reproductive years begin to fade, whether queer, straight or cisgender, we can experience our body and sexuality with more freedom. Explicit or unconscious expectations of our body's biological function hold less value once reproduction is off the agenda. Invariably, our bodies soften, weaken, grow or reduce with the natural process of ageing and through the hormonal changes of midlife. These changes may mean we are forced to confront our relationship with our body, and this may trigger long-held narratives and crises. For example, people who have lived with eating disorders in their past can become vulnerable to a relapse with the advent of middle age (Hodson, 2023). The young, gawky boy who found acceptance by training rigorously to become strong and sporty in his teens may feel lessened or ashamed when his muscular physique and physical strength reduce. We may experience loss and a shifting identity as the body that has housed us thus far in life now starts to change in ways we cannot control.

Arguably, heteronormative narratives of sexual activity and function need not constrain people as they move beyond their sexually reproductive years. This means that straight sex can become more like queer sex, which has never had a reproductive focus and therefore, arguably, has explored more inventiveness. Changes in sex hormones can mean vaginal dryness, lack of energy and low libido for many women. For men, it can lead to fatigue and listlessness, as well as a lack of libido. Cisgender women may no longer want penetrative sex, not only because it can be more painful but also because it is no longer biologically necessary. A new landscape opens up for exploration. Indeed, as Germaine Greer summarises in *The Change* (1991/2018), intercourse is not the only way to have sex. Intimacy, tenderness and emotional pleasure can be just as rewarding, and women may experience more sexual freedom as a result. Feminist, gender and sexuality scholar Kelsey Henry concludes from her research (2015) that all growing old is queer as we attempt to 'unbecome' and 'rebecome' ourselves, circling back and playing with old narratives.

There have been theories (usually hypothesised by men) about the connection between women's fertility and sex for aeons. They began with the Hippocratics in the third century BC, and their theory of the four bodily humours – blood, phlegm, yellow bile and melancholy. These four humours were understood to define people's physical and mental health, and personality as well. The interaction of the four humours explained differences of age, gender, emotions and disposition, and they changed with the seasons and times of day, and across the life span. As feminist cultural historian Elinor Cleghorn tells us in her incisive investigation of the many ways in which traditional Western medicine has failed women (2021), it is still anchored in part by beliefs set out by the ancients and out-of-date science. She shows us how views on female sexuality, while diverse and complex, generally peddled the idea that women were less sexually interested than men and that their reproductive organs were the primary influence on their sexual behaviour. Further, they proposed that women were naturally passive and submissive in sexual matters and had a weaker sex drive than men.

Why the history lesson? Because these theories prevailed in some guise until the emergence of empirical science in the mid-19th century, and they are dangerous for women's health, especially as they were based on incomplete or erroneous information about women's bodies and sexual experiences. They have been equally devastating for a woman's relationship with her body. Menopause began to be conceptualised in the mid-16th century, with mentions of symptoms such as hot flushes, joint pain, sweats and, notably, 'hysteric fits' (Appignanesi, 2008). Bloodletting was a popular treatment, again based on the idea that, once her periods ceased, a woman had too much 'blood' humour in the body, and it needed to be released. Medical writing in the 17th century was the first to conceptualise and treat menopause as a specific disease. Purgatives and incarceration in the lunatic asylum were common treatments, as well as highly dangerous surgery to remove ovaries and the clitoris. Moving into the 19th century, morphine, laudanum and lead acetate injections into the vagina were added to the treatments on offer. The message was that something was very wrong with women's bodies.

As recently as 1916, William Blair Bell, Professor of Obstetrics and Gynaecology at Liverpool University and co-founder of the Royal College of Obstetricians and Gynaecologists, devised a menopause diagnosis loosely based on the endocrine system but overlaid with strongly publicised 'ideals of femininity'. He proposed that women who had high levels of hormones were over-sexualised, and those with feebler hormones were shrivelled and childless. The feminine ideal, we have to assume, was somewhere in between (Cleghorn, 2021). Once again, we can see how, in the public and medical discourse, a woman's relationship with her sexuality is bound up with her hormones and fertility, and social ideals and expectations of femininity. Arguably the prescription of HRT, starting from the 1960s, with significant economic gain for pharmaceutical companies, has perpetuated this. Although HRT is undoubtedly a saviour for women who are crippled by their menopause symptoms, the rhetoric around it still promotes the idea that it is returning a woman to her former self, including a resurgence of sexual desire, rather than making it more bearable for her to be as she is now. Holding this understanding can be very helpful when working alongside women in menopause in a counselling setting, as it forms a social, historic backdrop to their embodied existence.

Joanna was clearly feeling awkward as this part of our conversation opened up. It was clear in her words and in her body language – the way she folded in and scrunched herself up. I persisted, testing the boundaries to see if something new could be revealed while trying to be respectful and careful. In her initial assessment, Joanna hadn't disclosed any specific trauma or distress related to sex, but that didn't mean it wasn't there. 'It feels hard for you to relate to yourself that way...' I began, tentatively. 'Yeah, it's not that I don't want to, it's just that I don't know how to, I guess,' she replied.

'So, it feels strange and new?' She nodded.

'Do you want to give it a bit of space here, if it feels safe?' I asked.

She laughed. 'Ha! I bet you weren't expecting to talk about sex today, at least not with me, right?' Her humour briefly released the tension.

I smiled. 'So, it feels strange to think of yourself as sexual and yet just now I heard you say, even in passing, that you might like to spend the night with someone other than your husband. I am curious what is behind that, if you have a hunch.'

I invited her to feel this into her body, rather than think it through cognitively. I suggested grounding herself on the floor and in the chair first – bringing her legs out from under her, placing her feet on the floor and her palms on her thighs. I mirrored her with my posture. She let her gaze drop, absorbed in thought, but with her body more open than previously in the session.

'Erm... I suppose my body feels different now. I feel like I am missing out on something and... no it's more than that... I feel like I deserve something that I am not getting.' She paused. Then she went on, 'Honestly, he bores me. It's always the same. I haven't been physically intimate with anyone else for over 25 years. Crikey, that sounds weird, doesn't it? And, yeah, it's definitely my body, not my mind, responding that way.' At that, she sat back, pensive. 'Huh,' she said, assimilating what she had just said.

Freud had controversial views on women, believing that their lives were dominated by their sexual reproductive functions. He believed that girls had penis envy, so they either mimicked men by becoming actively sexualised or settled into a passive role and replaced their need for a penis with a desire to have a child (1925/1927). His theory was based on a model where femininity only existed in relation to masculinity. This is precisely the model that Simone de Beauvoir attempted to deconstruct in *The Second Sex*, published in 1949, and female psychiatrists have also subsequently challenged (Lehmann, 2001). Freud was also, according to Lisa Appignanesi, author of *Mad, Bad and Sad* (2008), 'a firm believer that the birth of a child would sort out many women's hysterical and neurotic impulses' (p.198). While Freud wrote many of these things within a specific social context and while conducting his research and formulating his ideas, they quickly became codified into norms by psychoanalysts and were used to stigmatise and pathologise women. As Appignanesi records, the archetypes of the frigid, hysterical and nymphomaniac woman were recognisable in the post-war era and beyond.

These archetypes still haunt women today. Our sexually reproductive years and our sex lives are closely connected, in common perception and in medical science. What might it be about older women that gives people a hard time conceptualising them as sexual? Older women's sexual desire is often stigmatised or overlooked in popular culture. In his review of the film *Good Luck to You, Leo Grande*, in which a retired woman hires the services of a younger male sex worker, the *Observer* film critic Mark Kermode concluded that it was 'admirably subversive… but not quite believable' (Kermode, 2022). How often in modern film or literature do we see ageing women's sexuality celebrated? How tragic to see it so carelessly dismissed. Are we surprised that a man found the premise of an older woman hiring a young sex worker to meet her sexual needs 'not quite believable'? It is more usual to see older women's sexuality depicted in a tragic or dysfunctional way. Look at Blanche Dubois in the Tennessee Williams play *A Streetcar Named Desire* (1947/2009). An ageing, fading Southern belle, Dubois deploys her sexuality to manipulate men, struggling to maintain a facade of beauty and youth. The characterisation mirrors the societal expectations placed on women to conform to restrictive standards of beauty and youthfulness, and, lacking all else, their use of their sexuality as a means of gaining power or social status. Such women are also victim of the double standard that exists in society, where men of any age are admired for their sexual exploits, while women are shamed for theirs. Try to imagine the public reaction if former Prime Minister Theresa May had begun a relationship with a younger beau; then think of Donald Trump (if you can bear to do either, of course).

'That sounded weird to hear myself say I have needs,' Joanna exclaimed. She seemed to be hearing a voice that transcended her own usual narrative. However, she didn't seem ready to accept it just yet. 'It seems a bit seedy, doesn't it?'

I reflected that back to her: 'It seems seedy for you to have needs?' Shame is no stranger to women; we are used to hiding and being embarrassed about menstruation, fertility, motherhood, menopause, growing old and having sexual desires.

'Hmmm, well, sex was never about me really when I first started out, you see; it was a route into or out of something,' Joanna explained. 'I was always either running away or trying to fit in or trying to be something. I was actually quite good at it I suppose.' Her hands flew up to her face momentarily as she said this last bit, suddenly embarrassed. 'And, well, it seemed to bring me what I needed, which again sounds bad to me.'

I was aware of how uncomfortable she seemed to be feeling. 'Joanna, you seem to feel awkward talking about this, I can see you are holding yourself quite stiffly and you were almost hiding your face with your hands just now. I am wondering what's happening in your body?'

Joanna closed her eyes and listened in. She breathed a deep breath, trying to access what she might be experiencing. 'Honestly, nothing is coming to me,' she replied. 'I actually don't really feel "in" my body as I am talking to you at all, which is weird.' I wondered if Joanna was avoiding feeling something or not ready to feel what was there. I decided to go carefully. The philosopher Merleau-Ponty (1945/2002) maintained that our body isn't something we own; we *are our body*. And our embodied experience is entangled in our experience of other people and the exigencies of relating. This idea can be very helpful in the therapeutic encounter, as represented in the theory and practice of Gestalt (Perls, 1969), and focusing (Madison, 2014), among others. Even when people can't feel anything, there will be a sensation that holds clues. 'Okay, let's go with that,' I said. 'What is it like *not* to feel in your body?'

'Safe, I suppose.' Said very quietly, in a small voice now.

'Safe from…?'

'Safe from what you might think of me.' Joanna paused. 'And what I might feel about what you think.'

'Okay,' I summarised. 'So let's see if I've got this right. Talking about sex makes you jump outside your body so you can protect yourself from whatever you might feel and from what others might feel. Does that feel right?'

At this Joanna nodded vehemently and smiled ruefully. 'Yep, and you know what?' Here she almost shouted. '*That* is exactly what happens to me when I have sex. Always has done. I'm never in my body, I am always watching to see what happens and how the person I am with is reacting. I'm like a stranger in my body.'

In our time together up until this point, we had roamed through many of Joanna's life events and relationships. She was one of two siblings, growing up in a working-class household in rural Wales. Her older sister was severely disabled and much of her parents' time and energy was spent facilitating her sister's care. Her mother stayed at home and could not work as a result. Joanna left home for secretarial college at the age of 16, staying with distant relatives in a town many miles from her home. She struggled to make friends and fit in at the large accountancy firm where she found part-time work. Her parents rarely contacted her to check on her – they were too absorbed in the care of her sister and her father worked long hours. Joanna had told me she had to grow up very quickly and, although she hadn't ever felt unsafe or specifically pressured, sex became an easy way to form connections and be accepted.

'There was a big group of us from college, and from the other colleges nearby. It seemed to me that everyone was dating or seeing someone.' She explained how this all became part of the social currency and a way of fitting in. 'I was grateful for the company, I suppose. Everyone seemed so glamorous. I felt I was really only play-acting.'

While we were talking about her body now, I remembered those conversations about when she was younger. 'So, this body of yours,' and here I gently held out my hand, palm turned up, 'is used to just showing up, maybe, and not really feeling what is going on...'

'Yes,' affirmed Joanna quietly.

I continued. 'If we offer it a little attention here, now...' I brought my hand to rest over my own heart and nodded for Joanna to do the same, 'I wonder if it has anything to say about that.' We both sat a while, eyes closed and each with a hand on our heart-space. I breathed deeply and slowly and waited in silence to see if anything came to Joanna.

She giggled a little and swallowed the sound. 'I am so not used to asking my body stuff, it's weird,' she said, and then waited again, listening. 'If it is saying anything, I think it is saying, "What about me?" Also, I feel as if there's maybe a little fire somewhere that wants some air in order to burn brighter, but maybe I am just saying that because I think that's what I am supposed to say in a counselling room?'

We both opened our eyes but kept our hands in contact with our bodies. I didn't want us to lose the moment, so I continued the thread a little. 'Even if that is what you think you should say, does it hold any truth?' She considered this. 'Well, yes. I mean I could be talking about pleasure, I suppose, or desire.'

'And do those words have any resonance?' I encouraged her to say more.

'Well, they are quite alien to me. It would be new, I suppose.'

And here I laughed. 'And you do seem a little confused by that as you say it.'

Joanna considered this for a bit and then, slightly incongruently, asked me, 'Is it normal, do you think, to not want other people to be attracted to you?'

I blinked, slightly taken aback by this change of direction, and asked her to say more.

'Well, I've noticed I don't like comments that my husband makes about how nice I look and everything, and at parties and when we are out, I used to notice people noticing me. I liked it, but now I couldn't care less, it irritates me.'

I felt compelled not to answer as it felt less like a question for me than an external expression of an important inner dialogue. I tried to stay still and allow this to emerge, but Joanna seemed still to be wanting my opinion. So I asked, 'And what do you make of that?'

'Well, I'm trying to put it all together. I have to admit I am a little confused now as we have moved around a bit in our session today, but what I think I think, if you see what I mean, is that I would like my body to experience pleasure and I don't particularly need that to be with anyone else?'

There is a widespread belief that sex becomes an issue for some women in menopause, but this is arguably an illusion created by popular images and ideas, not always borne out in reality. Writer Heather Corinna suggests: 'Menopause more often seems a highly convenient scapegoat than the actual source of the problem' (2021, p.217). The significant decrease in oestrogen and progesterone levels in menopause can undoubtedly bring about physical and emotional changes that may affect a woman's sexuality. It can lead to physical discomfort or pain during intercourse, or a lack of confidence or energy that might limit a woman's ability or motivation to be sexually intimate. The same hormone changes can also cause decreased libido and difficulty achieving orgasm (NHS Inform, 2023a). Yet, this can be compounded further by psychological and social changes that are associated with ageing, such as body image concerns, relationship issues and life stress. The ageism that is rampant in the media can also contribute to a decreased ability to enjoy sexual activity. The cultural rhetoric (and that of the multi-million-pound beauty and cosmetic industry) places value on improbable standards of youthful physical appearance and slimness in older women (Hofmeier et al., 2017). Against this backdrop, self-image and appreciation can suffer, and these are often very important ingredients of intimacy and sexual enjoyment.

However, here too it is important not to generalise and to note that not all women experience negative sexual changes or feel negative towards their body during menopause. Existential philosopher and psychotherapist Emmy van Deurzen sees midlife as a gateway to empowerment for women. 'We are too busy with our femininity for a long time due to our biology,' she told me when I talked to her in my research for this book. 'Somewhere along the line, both men and women will judge us on our attractiveness or our cuteness and for our ability to mother. As women, we bring these to the surface and make huge efforts to make them shine through… and that's a lot of work!' According to van Deurzen, once women become free of their biological burden, they can rebel and reinvent themselves. She argues that the post-menopausal years in fact represent a long period of time during which we are freed from many burdens. 'This is about claiming that strength of character, a new authority in the world. We are more angular, square, aware of things not mattering. We become more equal with men,' she told me.

Indeed, there is even a recognition that a woman becomes more 'male' in her post-menopausal years. Gynaecologist Robert Wilson, in his 1966 book *Feminine Forever*, called post-menopausal women 'castrates', and psychiatrist David Reuben reflected in his popular but controversial book *Everything You Always Wanted to Know about Sex* (*But Were Afraid to Ask)* (1969) that women in midlife time were dysfunctional as women and therefore very close to being a man. However inflammatory that is to read, the essence of what these two men are expressing is a certain freedom from biological imperative.

It is worth mentioning again that the overriding menopause narrative reinforces heterosexual norms, which not only isolates those that don't align to them but also closes down any idea of 'otherness', or any sexual experiences that deviate from heterosexual, penetrative sex. Yet older women are portrayed on television as 'sexless beings who fall outside regulatory norms of gender identification' and are therefore queered or othered from a gender standpoint anyway (Cooper, 2008, p.35). As psychotherapist and writer Tania Glyde concludes in their thesis on queer experiences of menopause, women become less gendered, and therefore less 'binary', as the female hormones decline. In fact, they argue, cisgender women may no longer want penetrative sex and may therefore explore new ways of engaging in pleasure (Glyde, 2023). It is also argued that non-reproductive sex is boundless and therefore creates fear in mainstream, normative society, and this fear is indisputably what is behind homophobia, transphobia and anti-contraception and abortion attitudes (Corinna, 2021). Glyde, in their research, concluded that counsellors should listen without making assumptions. I would add that counsellors should be undertaking continuing professional development around gender, sex and relationship diversity and how these are impacted by identity, menopause and hormones. With all menopausal clients, queer or straight, we must remain vigilant to heteronormal narratives in our language and open the dialogue to explore a client's lived reality of their body, identity and needs beyond the norms.

And, indeed, in my own research, I found that menopause and freedom from their reproductive biology has given many women an opportunity to experience their bodies in a new way, free of expectation. Some women may find that their libido increases, or that they experience more intense orgasms or seek out different ways of finding pleasure. I have spoken to many women who have found a sense of personal freedom and strength during and after menopause that allowed them to break out of usual ways of being and explore a different relationship with their body. Liz, café owner and part-time singer, told me that, initially, her body changed almost beyond recognition. She gained weight, her libido disappeared almost overnight, and she didn't have the energy to go running – her one solace in a very demanding job and personal life. She felt crushing self-consciousness, both socially and, most devastatingly, with her husband. This was her second marriage and it had always been strongly sexual, with regular intimacy. She confided in a friend, who suggested she seek counselling, and through that journey she began to rebuild her confidence again, which made all the difference in her relationship. 'I have now found an inner pride to be me and all that I am. What became transformational for me was the realisation dawning that I had fewer years in front of me than behind me, and I was spending all this time hiding from people, hiding from myself even. What for?' It was important to Liz that she found this pride inside herself, rather than from external validation. This wasn't about looking younger; it was about a deep appreciation for herself in any form. Sex is after all, about our whole self (Corinna, 2021). 'And then, do you know what, weirdly sex has been better than it was before, and more varied,' she told me. 'I kind of think, I deserve everything! I am much more demanding, far less demure!'

Studies show that societal attitudes towards sex in midlife affect our sexual behaviour. However, they also conclude that, in some non-industrial societies, older women are less inhibited and more powerful and sexually active (Leventhal, 2000). This is quite a different viewpoint to the deficiency model that is perpetuated in the Westernised world. The paradigm of deficiency in midlife is not the sole reserve of women;

the archetype of a diminished middle-aged man with little passion or drive is rife within social and cultural discourse. In the early 20th century, doctors experimented with controversial therapies (the early precursors to Viagra, if you will) to help return men of a certain age to their former vigour. Freud and the poet William Butler Yeats were among those who underwent the 'reactivation' procedure – essentially a vasectomy, innovated by biologist Eugen Steinbach (MUVS, 2016). Many of these reactivation therapies were then adapted for ageing women (Cleghorn, 2021), with limited outcomes and, in some cases, disastrous consequences, as it involved x-rays on and sometimes removal of the uterus, leading to sudden menopause. However dangerous, these influential ideas informed modern pharmaceutical advancements from the 1960s onwards that perpetuated the idea that what a person desires in middle age is to bring back something that has been lost, rather than move forward with what is present now. I rather think it stands to reason that women who engage in a journey of self-discovery, which counselling can support, could break out of these societal norms and find their own way of being. I sensed that Joanna might be on such a journey.

Joanna had identified that her body might be yearning for something more, but this wasn't yet a conscious thought, or at least not yet one that was integrated into her lived experience of herself. She had used the words 'pleasure' and 'desire' in quite a detached way: 'Well, yes, I mean I could be talking about pleasure I suppose, or desire.' I was curious about what they meant for her.

'I don't really associate them with me,' Joanna said. The statement felt quite final, definite.

'Who do you associate them with, if not you?' I continued.

Here, Joanna became quite animated, warming to her theme as she developed it. 'I see younger women dressing a certain way as if they are drawing people in, wanting them to be attracted to them. It seems quite transparent. And I know I used to do this. I was slim, I was always told I was attractive, and I was small, and I think a way of me being bigger was to try and be seen for my looks, you know. I am actually kind of ashamed of that now.' Again, her hands flew to her face briefly as if to hide from my gaze, or her own judgement. 'Honestly, it sounds awful to think I used to do that. It's appalling.' As we paused for her to consider her feelings on this, I couldn't help but notice how we had travelled in those few moments from desire and pleasure to shame in a very short leap. Was this, I wondered, why Joanna didn't feel able to connect with those feelings?

I shared this with Joanna. 'Yeah, I suppose desire is something that I see as quite selfish. You are kind of manipulating other people to get what you want.'

'So let me get this right – experiencing your own desire and pleasure is manipulative and perhaps a little shameful?'

'Yes, I guess,' Joanna replied, but she didn't sound sure.

'And as you are talking about them now, do you feel ashamed?'

'Well, no, not really.' I invited Joanna to think about what other responses she might have to these ideas, playfully at first. 'Hmmm, I want them to mean personal power. I want them to mean something wonderful, like when you really crave a food and then you finally have it, and it feels good. That's what you always read about, don't you?'

In this particular session we had been exploring her relationship with her husband and we had meandered at first, and then walked more purposefully towards discussing her sexuality. However, in many other sessions, Joanna had been gradually formulating her experience of being an almost post-menopausal woman. She'd found solace in literature, in therapeutic groups in nature, in reading myth and feminist writings. She loved the metaphors she was developing for her own menopause, especially that of a deep vein of wisdom and empowerment that she felt connected to, that pulsed within all menopausal women. I was curious about how this experiencing of herself might connect with her sexual self. I had a chance to bring this into our conversation when she mentioned personal power. How might this 'pulsing vein' with which she identified fit with her ideas of passion?

'Well, it empowers me to go and get what I need, to be sure of myself, to be independent and not need to use my body to serve other people. My body is here to serve me,' she said.

I uttered an involuntary, but hopefully affirming 'Amen' at this last sentence.

We had been actively working with Joanna's ability to respond to others in a way that considered her own needs as well as theirs. Growing up in a home with a lot of conflict, she had learnt that her safety lay in adapting to what was being asked of her so as to cause the least friction and attract the least attention. It was partly this dynamic that meant she had been largely diplomatic and compliant within her marriage. In our counselling relationship, it had shown up when we discussed dates and times for our sessions. Joanna would seem to accept whatever I offered, even if it meant making her life more complicated to work around the logistics. We'd noted this early on in our relationship and agreed to regularly check it out. While this compliance had served Joanna in one way, by keeping her safe, it didn't serve her in others. Specifically, it meant her needs were ignored. At a time when her resources were being stretched, caring and worrying for two sick parents, ignoring her own needs became harmful to her health and mental health. I knew Joanna came to counselling for this to be different.

'Okay,' I took a deep breath, 'how are we doing?' We were coming to the end of our session, and I wanted to check in on how she was feeling but also what she had heard. My 'Amen' to her last comments had laid bare my commitment to her finding a new way of being, but she might not be there yet. I have a tendency to want to feel that something of value has happened within the counselling space: that I can journey with people through their dilemmas into the experience of hope and knowing. This is actively and wisely held by my supervisor, and by my own 'internal supervisor' when I'm with clients. I try to keep in mind the counsel from the legendary existential therapist Irvin Yalom, who says we can never know the healing factor in any given therapeutic experience, as clients find meaning and growth in ways we simply cannot anticipate (2015). People who come into counselling know themselves, even when they feel they don't, and even when society subtly casts them as vulnerable. Humanistic psychology views humans as growth-orientated, as always having the capacity for self-actualisation (Maslow, 1968; Rogers, 1951/2003). This means that, within the safety of a trusted therapeutic relationship, people can find out for themselves and tell us where their areas for growth are. As Joanna and I had been working hard to develop her own sense of herself, I didn't want to wrap this up in a neat package and finish it off with a tidy bow of my own understanding, as she might not have drawn the same awareness from our conversation.

'Well, I am not going to lie, I do find talking about sex a bit cringey,' Joanna explained, 'and earlier I really didn't want you to go there. I could feel myself pressing myself further and further into this chair, wishing I could get away from you!'

I smiled in half apology, and waited for what else might come. 'But what I am thinking now is that it might be time for me to do what makes me happy, sex-wise, and what brings me [here she made air quotes with her fingers] "pleasure", whatever that means. And not just having sex as a means to an end, because I feel I have to...' She left a small pause and then added, 'And I suppose that might be as good for my self-development as my outdoor walks or getting my boundaries better vocalised with my husband or friends.'

I nodded and then asked, 'And that feels right? You aren't saying that because you think that's what needs to be said?' I checked this out with her, in line with the agreement we'd made to regularly review her tendency towards compliance in the counselling relationship.

'No, it feels right.' Again, Joanna placed both feet on the floor and breathed in, taking in what she'd said. She seemed to be asking this question of her body and was gazing into the middle distance above my head while she did. 'No, yes, it feels right,' she said with a small, decisive nod, 'It feels good actually.'

We both took a breath as the session came to a close. Joanna unfolded her diminutive frame from the chair and leaned down to return her shoes to her feet. As she stood to leave, she quipped, with a wink, 'Unless, of course, it all just means that I want to have sex in a hotel room with someone else and it really is just that straightforward.'

When clients come into counselling, our role as counsellors is to support them to intimately know their psychological and emotional landscape so that they can be mindful, rather than mindless, towards their sense of self. Their embodied experience in the world is as important as, and inexorably connected to, that landscape. Being watchful of how you are experiencing someone in the room with you can help reveal something they weren't aware of. In my first stint of personal therapy during my training, the therapist I worked with was unflinching in this respect. It made me relatively uncomfortable at the time – which, I am sure, she was aware of and spurred her on further. However, this attention to my body revealed something small but significant: when we were nearing something I was avoiding, or nearing the end of our session, the foot on my crossed leg would angle itself towards the door. It seemed to do it of its own accord

– certainly, I wasn't conscious of driving it. It was, as the therapist observed with painful acuity, a signpost to some of the necessary destinations for my journey into all parts of myself.

Menopause is an embodied experience; it is one of several transitions in a woman's life where physiology and psychology collide so that her identity can be irreversibly changed, opening up new parts of ourselves and closing others. Sexuality is intimately connected with this experience, precisely because, at least in heteronormal narratives, female sexuality is connected to reproduction. The possibility that a woman emerges from her menopause with a stronger sense of her embodied self, of her own body's desires and boundaries, and an urge to exist for herself, rather than for others, is an exciting one. It is a possibility that needs to be carefully nurtured, as embodied experiences also carry echoes of the past, as with Joanna's story.

All psychotherapists, regardless of our modality, and perhaps all practitioners in the healthcare and helping professions in general, must commit at the heart of our work to explore what clients would like to be different in their lives and to believe that they can achieve this. Our role as counsellors is to be aware of the inescapable medical, social and cultural filters that may have weighed on a woman's life and body, and on our own; to be aware of the stereotypes and work to transcend them by finding and experiencing this unique person in the room. The easiest way to do this is to be curious, to hold the space open for stories to emerge, to notice how we feel in relation to this person, and then to explore this holistic landscape, with all its myriad elements, together. This is true even when – especially when – it feels uncomfortable and strange. As Emmy van Deurzen argues (2012), true psychotherapy is orientated not towards the actuality of our clients but towards their potentiality:

> It is only then that they discover, with surprise and wonder, that in spite of all their distress, worry and suffering, life is ultimately full of promise and eminently worth the effort of living it. (p.238)

The uncomfortable and strange will undoubtedly lead to something new.

Chapter 4
Back to the future

We are all travellers in the wilderness of the world and the best
we can find in our travels is an honest friend.
Robert Louis Stevenson, *Travels with a Donkey* (1879/1915)

Summer had arrived with potency; the air in my thankfully well-
shaded counselling room at home was still and heavy. A fan quietly
whirred, sweeping a disruptive and feeble breeze through the room.
As the temperature rose, I found that sitting very still allowed me
not to get too hot or distracted from the work. Today I was meeting
George, a man in his late 50s who, in his own words, was 'on the brink
of an affair' and had found himself stuck in a dilemma of his own
making. We were three or four sessions in, and on this day he had
arrived a little late, a little flustered, and took some time to settle. His
hands were busy, dancing on the arms of his chair, fingers fluttering.
This wasn't unusual, but what was different were his clothes. Our
sessions were in the middle of the day, and he usually arrived smartly
dressed in a button-down shirt and jeans or chinos. Today he was in
jeans and a bright red French Connection t-shirt, with its ubiquitous
slogan loudly blazed across his chest: 'FCUK'.

I was holding myself still against the heat and listening intently.
George had been describing his frustration, palpable in his body
language, with the difference in libido between himself and Shirley,
his wife of 36 years. As I looked into his eyes, in my peripheral vision

the white capital letters of his t-shirt slogan mocked me. This didn't seem the right time to mention the paradox – though I thought it might come later.

'I understand she might not feel like having sex with me, I do understand that,' George stated. He was worrying at a fleck of fluff on the leg of his jeans and looking down, lost in thought.

'You used the word "understand" twice there,' I noted.

'Hmm,' he said and returned to bouncing his fist on the arm of the chair. I stayed silent.

'Well, I *say* I understand,' he eventually said, 'but I don't know why she can't just do it for my sake. She knows how important sex is to me, how important my needs are.' I felt a small flicker of anger at this, an identification with Shirley, and I registered it. I wondered why I felt I had to take sides. I reminded myself to stay with George and leaned in a little more.

'You feel undervalued somehow,' I ventured, gently.

'I just really need to have sex,' he said, 'and I think that gets lost at the moment.'

'Lost…?' I asked.

'She is so tired all the time, and work isn't going well. She wants to retire soon too. She never wants to go out, prefers being at home and in her own company and I feel like I am so patient and understanding and it's all we ever talk about.' He sighed, 'There's just no room for anything else.'

'No room for you.'

'Not really, no.' He laughed, 'And I don't need much, you see, I'd just like some hanky panky.'

Divorce rates among older age groups have been steadily climbing in the industrialised West, year on year. In the past 10 years, the average age at divorce recorded for England and Wales has risen from 43 years to 46 (Statistica, 2023). This increase in 'grey divorce', as it is known, is in marked contrast to the overall decline in divorce rates. According to one study, in the US, more than 25% of people who get divorced are aged 50 or older (Brown & Wright, 2019). Relationships of all sorts form a large part of the midlife transition, as they are essential to our connectedness to life and to our 'self' and can be influential or problematic as we go through any significant change. The co-existence of male and female experiences of midlife can create dilemmas as they are often so different in their essence. Within heterosexual relationships, this may also be influenced by a man's experience of living with a partner undergoing their menopausal journey, and vice versa. We also need to consider the impact of the male menopause as experienced by wives, female friends, family members and colleagues.

Midlife experience within same-sex relationships is no less liable to cause tension, as no one experiences this time of life in the same way, influenced and impacted as we are by our earlier life experiences, own identity and sense of self. While this discord can cause crisis, it can also be generative. There is thus a much greater richness of experience to the midlife 'crisis' than the unimaginative depictions of risk-taking men and tired, angry women. And how can it ever just be one-dimensional when our lives are so interconnected?

George was semi-retired; having worked in the middle ranks of the civil service his whole career, he had decided there was no future growth or potential for him there. He didn't have the appetite to start anything new jobwise now and, with his two children grown up and financially independent, he no longer felt the need to earn more for the family. He had recently become a governor at the local secondary school and devoted some of his free time to that. Through our initial conversations, I noticed his language was bland when he talked about most aspects of his life.

'Oh, you know, it's kind of a 9-to-5 job with no real drama,' he had said when I asked how he experienced his work. 'I just keep everything ticking over.'

'You enjoy it?' I ventured.

'It's kind of fine,' George had acknowledged.

'When you are talking today about your job, it feels to me all grey and misty. I can't seem to feel its form or where it fits in your life. I wonder, does it feel that way for you?' I remarked.

'Huh,' George replied, shrugging.

I shrugged my shoulders a little too, to sense how it felt, but also to mirror his experience, and left a silence.

'I guess I don't really care about it. I'm kind of bored.'

'You are bored,' I repeated.

'Yeah,' he sighed. I waited to see if anything more emerged.

'I'm bored with most things, I think,' he said, the tone of his voice descending to a full stop, and he demonstrated the sense of defeat with another shrug of his shoulders.

There is a theoretical argument in the field of gender equality studies that the increasing malaise among and declining mental health of men are impacted by the significant ground gained in recent decades by women. Writer and scholar Richard Reeves, author of the influential work *Of Boys and Men* (2022), asserts that the male role is socially constructed as that of provider, based on woman's historical dependence on him. Now that far fewer women are reliant on the male breadwinner, Reeves argues, this has created a deficit: men are no longer needed to play this traditional role but are not yet able to frame or inhabit a new one.

I see this represented at all ages and stages of life in different ways. The teenage son of one of my close friends spent some time talking to me about how he and his friends feel they are pushed into male stereotypes at school and on social media because of the rise of feminism among their female peers and the intense focus on equality at school. 'Every personal development lesson is about women's rights, and the patriarchy and men attacking women, and I get it, I really do, but this doesn't represent me. I shouldn't have to pay for what other generations of men have done,' he said. Clearly confused and angry, he told me, 'It's hard to find the right way to be.'

Middle age for men is often associated with a sense of loss of power and loss of place, in contrast to women's experience of discovering a new place in the world and new roles. Life transition researcher and writer Gail Sheehy reports on this in her landmark book on men's transitions, *Understanding Men's Passages*. In conversation with the psychoanalyst John Munder Ross, he tells her: 'Many women begin to look for positive changes in their forties and fifties, when their years of total parenthood are winding down... Men are much needier and more dependent... than we like to acknowledge' (1999, p.51). I discussed this with existential philosopher and psychotherapist Emmy van Deurzen, whose approach to therapy is characterised by a robust view that we bravely face into the dilemmas of life. Her view on men approaching midlife is similar: that they see it as an experience within which they are going to lose part of themselves, rather than gain, while women often find a new power through midlife and menopause transition. 'Men have believed that they must be tough and successful and competitive, and when they feel that is waning, it is very hard for them because they may feel there is nothing to replace it with. There is very little for them to "go towards", she told me. At a time when women, whether colleagues, friends or partners, are going through significant change, this may be disorientating, even disempowering for men, creating a new sense of malaise, and sometimes helplessness. For her, working therapeutically with men in midlife can be about helping them explore and discover their creativity and mellowness and encouraging them to form platonic, rather than sexual, bonds with others.

I had a feeling that something like this might be happening for George, but I couldn't yet get a sense of his experience as he was living it. We had a way to go.

'What does this boredom feel like within your body, as you talk about it now?' I placed my hand to my stomach here, to encourage him to feel into his own.

'Erm, I don't really know,' he replied.

'Any sensations, colours, or any part of your body you notice more than others,' I encouraged further. He briefly closed his eyes, and tilted his head side to side, appearing to listen in.

'Nothing,' he replied, opening them again and looking at me.

'There's no information there,' I stated.

'I just don't ever think about how things are in my body.' He laughed and shrugged.

'Well, if there is a "nothing" sensation there,' I said, 'how is that for you?'

'It's just bland – easy, I suppose'.

'Bland.'

'I like not having to feel.'

'Because feeling means…' I kept him moving forward a little.

'Too much.'

There seemed to be a dichotomy in what he was describing and feeling. On the one hand, he was bored, and yet if he stopped, became still and thought about it for a moment, he was in fact feeling too much. And he didn't seem to want to feel that.

'So, I wonder if the boredom you are experiencing and nothingness you feel is in fact a way of *not* feeling?' I continued.

'It could be…' he began.

'It might not be,' I offered, 'but does that feel right as I say it?'

'A little, yes,' he conceded.

'So, the "too much"... do you know what's inside those words?' I wanted George to find a way to feel into what was there safely and work out what it was taking him towards, but I knew we needed to do this gently.

George's wife, Shirley, was a secondary school teacher. He told me she was fun and outgoing, 'the life and soul of any party', he said. Together they had enjoyed rounds of dinner parties, themed nights at their local pub and family holidays in resorts, enjoying the entertainment and buzz, always making friends as they went. He told me that in recent years Shirley had become withdrawn, sometimes suffering with headaches and often cancelling social events or leaving early, saying she was tired. He was sympathetic in the way he described it to me, explaining that she worked hard, it was a tiring career and, with the children having left home for good, she was missing family life. George didn't specifically mention the menopause, and I didn't offer it, but it was clear that Shirley might be experiencing some change in herself.

'She is just so quiet, you know, not "her"', George told me as we explored this one day. 'She reads a lot, watches programmes on TV, spends time on her own more when she is not at work.'

'You worry about her?' I asked.

'Er, no, not really.' He paused for more thought. 'I've asked if she is depressed or sad and she says not. In fact, she says she is "content".' He formed air quotes with his hands.

I mirrored the action. 'You made quote marks around the word "content" – what does that mean for you?'

George rolled his eyes. 'Oh, she does lots of mindfulness and tries to do yoga every day. She's talking about going cold-water dipping. It's all a bit wholesome and new age for me.'

'You don't like it?'

'No, I just wish she would channel that energy somewhere else instead.'

I waited for a moment. George continued.

'Yeah, like channel it on me, I suppose. On us and our relationship.'

'So, it feels like she has turned inward a little, perhaps spending more time with herself and inside herself...'

'Exactly.'

'And you feel?'

'Annoyed, left out, I suppose.'

'Left out of?'

'Our life, her life,' he faltered and thought a moment. 'Her new life maybe.'

As we explored this further, George was surprised to find that, although he felt that what was troubling him was Shirley's lack of libido, what he was also feeling was rejection and isolation for other reasons too. The yoga, mindfulness and the quietness that he had described earlier originally felt like Shirley was becoming less of a person, less 'her', as he said, but his irritation was hiding what he came to identify as a kind of jealousy. His career was waning – winding down in a planned way but no longer progressing. His children and wife seemed to need him less, or at least not in the way they used to. So, on this hot summer's day, faced with the red t-shirt, I was curious as to what was different. I asked him.

'Something feels different about you today, George. You seem energised, buzzing even.'

'I feel it!' he exclaimed. I asked him to describe it to me, resisting asking why, at this stage. He hadn't offered any information, and I was respectful of that.

'I feel I can't sit still,' he said. 'I want to get moving with something.' His leg was jumping up and down as he said this.

'Your leg is jumping, like it's ready to run out of here,' I laughed in reply.

'I want to tell you something. Is it okay if I do?'

'This is your space. You can bring whatever feels right,' I said, spreading my hands, palms up, in invitation, and I reminded him about the confidentiality in our contract.

'Well, I've thought a lot since our last session, and I've joined a choir. It's brilliant. We meet twice a week, and we have a performance already coming up this weekend. I've always been able to sing, since school days, but never learned properly. I feel brilliant when I am singing, like really alive. I love the way, when we all sing, and there are about 30 or 40 of us, it feels so powerful and free.'

'That is so good to hear,' I encouraged, 'You said you felt you wanted something new in your life, and it sounds like it is really helping.'

At this, George leant forward towards me. 'I tell you what *is* helping more than anything,' he almost whispered, and he winked too, and I got a flash of George as a child, telling secrets to friends at school, eyes wide: 'There are a lot of women there.' At this, he sat back, crossed his arms and all-but nodded at me. Clearly, he wanted me to respond; it felt almost like a test. I breathed in and took a moment to respond.

'I want to make sure I understand the connection between how much you are enjoying the choir and the fact that there are women there,' I began gently. It felt hard to say anything without sounding like I was judging. And, despite my attempts to be careful, I felt it came out clumsily.

George seemed not to notice. Perhaps he wanted this question, as he flashed back quickly, 'Because I can flirt. I am one of the few men there, I'm still in my prime and I seem to get a lot of attention from women. It is nice. It's been so long since I've had that.'

I was struggling to stay with George and his experience of the world at this point. I could feel my unconditional regard slipping; I felt a sharp tug of irritation. A quick scan produced the age-old stereotypical image of the middle-aged man trading in his wife for a younger model. I found myself thinking, surely there was some other answer to the boredom we had been exploring? I made a mental note to take this to supervision and returned to our conversation.

'It feels good to be noticed,' I reflected back to him.

'Yes, damn right,' he emphasised with another nod of the head. Then he quickly followed it with, 'That's okay, right?'

'Was that a question for me, or for you?' I returned, gently.

'Ah… yes, it was for you.'

'It matters to you that I think it's okay?' I checked.

'Well, I think maybe it's *not* okay in some ways.' George looked up at the ceiling. 'I think about things, you know, doing things with these other women. At the end of the rehearsal the other night, I wanted to kiss one of them as we went out to our cars.'

'As you said that just then, you looked upwards, away from me.'

'I know, I feel really awkward saying it.'

I felt awkward with him saying it too. I decided to be open about this: 'It does feel a little awkward, I feel that too. I am wondering why.'

Urie Bronfenbrenner (1993) proposed his ecological systems theory to explain how human development is shaped by different levels of social systems. The microsystem encompasses direct, face-to-face relationships and environments like family and school that profoundly impact a child's development. The mesosystem refers to connections between different parts of your microsystem, like between home and work. The exosystem involves external environments that indirectly influence development, like communities and social structures. The macrosystem comprises overarching cultural values, laws and customs. Finally, the chronosystem is formed by the socio-historical events and transitions affecting an individual over their entire lifetime. According to Bronfenbrenner, these layered systems continuously interact throughout our lives to support and direct human growth. I find this a helpful model to have in mind when working with clients and to notice our own impact.

Counsellors mostly interact and have influence on our clients within the microsystem, in the microcosm of the therapeutic encounter. The physical and emotional space we hold for them becomes a stage on which they play out their lives. If we stay attuned to this, we can nurture the seeds of insight waiting to emerge and help rewrite this play. Our identity is always relational and historically situated, created by an ever-evolving and ongoing dialogue (Butler, 1990). Therefore, I feel that our role as counsellors is to introduce possibility and choice to our clients, rather than treating them as everyone else might. By introducing the opportunity of a different way of relating within the microcosm of the therapeutic dyad, we can challenge the experience in the macrocosm of the rest of the world (Bronfenbrenner, 1993).

Here, George was describing feeling something strong – an attraction to others that was a big part of the new-found excitement of singing in a choir. He had been bored for a while, and this new hobby was helping to alleviate that. On the one hand he was keen to tell me, feeling something new and exciting, yet something held him back. I had been keenly aware of George's version of Shirley's story in the background of our work: of her introspection and self-contentment, of his experience of her slowly moving away from him. I am a woman approaching middle age and I felt some affinity with Shirley, undoubtedly. This empathy with another person within the counselling space is not unusual. I took this to supervision, curious as to why it felt like this might be pulling me away from staying with George and his experiencing. The answer lay in the macrosystem, using the Bronfenbrenner model. George's pull towards the women he was meeting in a space of shared interest made sense in the context of what he was experiencing in his life at that time, but I had to recognise that my response was filtered through the stereotype of the middle-aged man seeking affairs, risk-taking and putting strain on their marriage. I had to recognise within me the sense almost of disappointment. This was just so typical, was it not? That was the source of the pull of irritation I had experienced when George began telling me about his desires. And if I wasn't careful, it would get in the way of our work together and hinder George's development and growth. What use was it if I was just another person seeking to impose my own social conditioning on him?

If I am truly honest, I think that this did get in the way of my work with George. As practitioners, we have to recognise that we don't always get it right. Supervision, reflective writing and personal therapy are the tools we use to tune into and work through what might be coming between us and the client we are with and their fulfilment and growth. I call this 'human soup' – the mix of individual and inter-relational experiences happening at any one moment within the therapeutic dyad. And, as with soup, it's hard to distinguish all the ingredients and flavours at play. If I reflect back on our work, it seemed that, from this point, we began to focus on one dilemma, one dynamic only: would he or wouldn't he have an affair? And then, when he did ultimately have an affair, would he or wouldn't he leave Shirley? I have long since wondered if my inability to reach across wholly into his world meant that we ended up in this binary pattern.

After my admission, 'It does feel a little awkward, I feel that too. I am wondering why,' we had both paused and reflected. I was immediately wondering if that had been too open or harsh and he was appearing to consider what I had said.

'You know what I think it is?' George began, and continued without waiting for me to answer, his words flowing quickly, freely and confidently, 'It's just not "me". Well, not the "me" people see. I have always been sensible and dependable. I worked hard, we had a good life as a family, the children got into good grammar schools and did well, we had two family holidays a year. I never get angry; I go with the flow – well, with three women in the house, I didn't have much choice with that one – and I rarely make big demands.' Here he stopped, deep in thought, lips pursed, and he ran his hand through his hair. I waited.

'Yeah, so people don't expect to me to be passionate and have desires.' His tone went down to a full stop at the end of this sentence, and he breathed out.

'People…' I noted his language, and this was both a statement and a question.

'Well, do you?' he challenged.

'Erm…' I was taken by surprise but knew this was the right question. 'Yes, I must admit I was taken aback a little by what you said. Maybe, because we have been talking a lot about your life, the one you just described, it seemed incongruous.' Here I paused, reflecting and wanting to create something for George that was helpful, then continued, 'But if I am honest, I think I was responding to you like anyone else might, perhaps judging you without realising it, but I recognise that what you need most from me is to see you, the real you, and what you are expressing. Not to stifle you. Don't you think?'

'Yeah, yeah, I do. Look, I just think I really want some good sex. Most people don't say that, do they, or at least admit it out loud,' George was in his flow now. 'And I am a bit tired of being dependable. I never used to be that way before I was married. In fact, I married Shirley when I did because I worried that I would never settle down and she was there and loved me.'

Something had undoubtedly shifted. Over the remainder of that session and others, we began to unpack these two sentences. Blurted out quickly and almost unthinkingly, they held so much within them. George made a connection between the sense of self that was emerging, out of awareness at first and then more obviously, from the responsibilities of his job, active fatherhood years and marriage, and the self he remembered from puberty until his mid-20s. He had grown up in west London; his father was a vicar, and his mother very much fulfilled the expected vicar's wife's role. Rebellious and bright, George left school for university a year early and spent four years in digs in central London, studying. During this time, he was part of the punk music scene and had a string of passionate but disconnected relationships. He visited his parents rarely, feeling little affinity with their stoicism and moderation.

I asked George if he liked his younger self, as he often smiled when he spoke about that time.

'Yeah, he was cool. I had fun, didn't take myself too seriously, everyone seemed to like me. I got loads of attention, I was really someone, you know.' I smiled back at him, feeling the strong connection he was experiencing with his younger self.

'I wonder, do you notice how the language you just used seems to mirror the language you use when you talk about how you feel now – wanting passion and enjoying being noticed and part of something?' I offered.

'Huh, yes, I suppose,' he answered. He didn't seem convinced. I wondered why it felt important to me that he should agree. It felt like we were at odds, and not for the first time.

'Maybe that connection feels too obvious, not right in some way?' I suggested. 'I suppose the reason I noticed it was that it felt to me like that younger part of you has always been there and feels more present now than it might have been in the past 30 years.' This seemed to trigger a thought. George went on to tell me that he always knew he had to settle down; his model for marriage and 'grown-up' life was what his parents had instilled in him. He felt that university was his time to rebel but that he always intended to settle down afterwards and take his place in the more conventional world of his parents' expectations.

Within Gestalt philosophy and theory, originated by Fritz Perls, the need that is uppermost in a person's experience is the 'figure'; it is all they can see. The theory proposes that we search around for a way to fulfil or answer that need and, when we find it, the need retreats into the background again (Perls, 1969). You will often hear this referred to in therapy, and in popular vernacular, as 'unfinished business', but it is so much more than that. Perls goes on to say that, when we experience a dissonance between our social experience (in George's case, his dependable life), and our biological experience (in George's case, his passionate self), the 'organism' (i.e. us) will eventually resolve it and focus on what is right for us. Most of us, Perls says, try to actualise what we should be, rather than be true to ourselves. And therapy is a place where we can notice this and resolve the dilemma – and never more so than in midlife, which, as developmental psychologists Erikson and Erikson (1998) so brilliantly put it, is a stage when we are asking ourselves big questions such as 'Has it all been worth it?' and 'Who am I now?' Essentially, we are rediscovering our 'I'.

'You mentioned inevitability… I'm not sure if you believe in fate at all, but that word seemed to imply that it wasn't your choice in some way,' I said in one session when George was talking about his decision to get married.

'Do you know, I think it was a choice, but I honestly don't think I thought about it too much. I was young, it seemed logical and so we did it.'

'You loved each other too?' I clarified.

'As much as I love anyone,' he said. 'I just don't think I feel that deeply. And you probably think that says something bad about me, but it's the truth. Apart from my children, I am not sure I really, truly love anyone else.' I began to respond, but he cut me off, laughing, 'And yes, before you ask me, I am totally okay with that. I've always known that. Being with Shirley was about sex originally, then companionship and children and being with someone, not about love. I am pretty sure she knows that and feels the same way.'

'You know, George, what I hear is that you are comfortable and familiar with this part of yourself, and I hope you know that I wouldn't ever feel that anything you say implies anything "bad". It feels very real when you express this.' I said this to reassure him, but also to mark what I was feeling, which was that he felt more authentic to me in that moment than at any other time in all the hours we had spent together. Yet I couldn't help feeling we were missing something, or that a part of him wasn't present in his story of logic and duty.

Remember George's t-shirt at the start of this chapter? I wonder if that, and George's sex-related dilemma that he brought to counselling, became a red herring – misdirection, as it were. Our work together ended abruptly when George became frustrated that he couldn't reach a decision about his relationships and decided to take a break to think. He never returned. Towards the end of our work, too late in some ways, I became curious about whether what George was actually experiencing might be related to his 'existence', to an awareness of his mortality rather than to his relationship to sex. I am an existentially informed therapist and the philosophy that underpins this approach is rooted in the idea that the understanding that we will one day die forms one of the greatest, if not the only, dilemma of our life. How do we live knowing life itself will one day be over? Not knowing when that will happen creates an anxiety that is with us throughout life, mostly out of our awareness. One of the greatest existential philosophers, Jean-Paul Sartre, argued that we spend much of our lives living in 'bad faith', attempting to avoid the responsibility of discovering our own authentic self (1956/2003). As I reflect now on the person George described himself being in his 20s, who seemed to be emerging once more in his midlife, I wonder, which was his most authentic self?

The existential therapy approach maintains that acknowledging the ultimate ending that is death can allow us to find meaning in our life (Spinelli, 2006). Certainly, in my work with older adults approaching the final years of life, I find that exploring our relationship with death can help people live more fully in life and release a sense of freedom. Working in this way has also profoundly changed me. As I wrote in my first book (Kewell, 2019): 'Sitting with a 95-year-old man exploring the meaning of his death taught me more about life than any book ever could' (p.127).

When I reflect again on this in the context of my work with George, I think perhaps some of the clues were there all along. It was there in the dilemma that brought him to counselling in the first place – an unease with how he was feeling, a sense that he had lost connection with his true self and boredom with how his life was now. Perhaps immersing himself in a dutiful life was a way of establishing legacy and progeny, an anchor into this world that would outlive him, an extension of the world his parents lived within? Perhaps the rebellious, vibrant self from his youth that reappeared in his midlife, the one that craved excitement and intimacy and to be seen, was his true self – an expression of the dizzying freedom of being human? As the eminent existential therapist and writer Irvin Yalom writes in *Staring at the Sun*, his book on overcoming death anxiety (2011):

> The fear of death creates problems that at first may not seem directly related to mortality. Death has a long reach, with an impact that is often concealed… often the fear is covert and expressed in symptoms that appear to have nothing to do with one's mortality. (p.7)

I regret deeply that George and I did not get to explore this in more detail. I believe that we practitioners should have the courage to challenge ourselves to acknowledge when we may have overlooked a dynamic or been pulled away from, or even swerved around, a process that was happening before our eyes. There are, of course, always reasons for this. Sometimes the avoidance by a client of parts of their experiencing is so strong and well-crafted that we are unable to discern it too. In systemic therapy, however, resistance does not belong to the client we are working with; it is a by-product of the relationship. We counsellors have a responsibility to notice the patterns we are being pulled into and notice where we are not going, so we can help our clients create something different or something new to happen for them (Bott & Howard, 2012).

As I come to the end of this account about my work with George, I should say that, for reasons I still haven't quite resolved, the sudden ending left me curious about Shirley's story. Undoubtedly, a good part of me resonated with what I learnt about her, but what stays with me still is the sense that midlife transition is so powerfully different for everyone. We can be journeying with someone through life and still transition independently, pulling against the current of the other's flow at critical times. Even our bodies experience this transition differently. I spoke with Nicci Parry, an integrated health and yoga practitioner and spiritual healer who specialises in midlife and menopause. I wanted to get a sense of how this middle-of-life transition impacts people across all dimensions, and what can help beyond talking therapy. She told me that men normally come to her seeking holistic support with a specific physical pain or muscular skeletal problem, which may lead them into work on themselves and their body more widely. Women, by contrast, tend to present seeking help with emotional and holistic problems, such as feeling overwhelmed and wanting to be in tune with their body. George was expressing that he wanted to be 'more'; his focus was largely external and his energy 'out' with others, seeking connection. Shirley, from his accounts of her at least, was focusing inwards, gathering her own resources from within, retreating a little from her outward responsibilities and interactions. I am not a couples therapist but I can imagine that relational therapy at such a pivotal time of life must be rich and challenging in equal measure for this reason alone.

Navigating your own transition can be demanding, confusing even. However, to do that successfully alongside or even in lockstep with someone else is a tough landscape to traverse.

Chapter 5
Counsellor, health thyself

All that you touch
You Change
All that you Change
Changes you. The only lasting truth
is Change.
Octavia E. Butler, *Parable of the Sower* (1993, p.3)

The last thing I wanted was infinite security and to be the place
an arrow shoots off from. I wanted change and excitement and
to shoot off in all directions myself, like the colored arrows
from a Fourth of July rocket.
Sylvia Plath, *The Bell Jar* (1963/2001, p.79)

My menopausal transition didn't so much as whisper its arrival on
the threshold of my approaching midlife stage; it sneaked through
the last few millimetres of space as the door to my youth closed
behind me, without me noticing. It then lay in wait, biding its time.
Sure, there were some physical signs that I was getting older, and my
cycle was undoubtedly changing, but I was on the lookout for the
usual symptoms: hot flushes, insomnia, becoming forgetful. What I
in fact first experienced was more of an inward, primal pull towards
something I couldn't name, long before the actual symptoms came
on.

Initially I found I was challenging myself more. I had noticed how my three children, all in secondary school, were being expected to learn new things every day and at a dizzying pace. On top of this, they were having to deal with experiences they found frightening or pressurising – dance competitions, sports matches – and I noticed I was telling them, 'It will build your resilience!' and 'Don't worry about being scared, it is your body's way of preparing you to succeed.' It began to dawn on me that I had not put myself out of my own comfort zone for a long time. Ah, the luxury of being an adult, in charge of your own existence and able to avoid the things that make you uncomfortable. So, I asked myself: What makes you scared? The answer was open water. I am a strong swimmer, swimming for my local and university teams in my youth, but the thought of swimming in wild, open water both fascinated and terrified me in equal measure.

Hence, two years ago, on a chilly April morning, I found myself in a wetsuit, toes dipped into the shallow waters of an iridescent, improbably deep, green lake. I swam the first and only mini-lap holding my breath, and with my eyes tightly shut inside my redundant goggles every time my face entered the water. Each sound, each movement within my peripheral vision fed my over-active imagination. It was pure terror, and so cold that my head hurt. But when I left the water exactly 14 minutes later, stood barefoot on the sandy bank and contorted myself out of my kit and into mercifully warm, dry clothes, I began to brim with euphoria. My body felt renewed by the cold, but it was more than that: I felt an enormous sense of achievement. I hadn't quite conquered my fears, but I had firmly shown them who was boss. My younger self metaphorically high-fived this slightly less brave older self.

One other experience stands out. I was spectating a rugby game. It was a harsh, wet Sunday in autumn. Mostly we were parents; most of those around me were fathers. The ground was hard, and the air thick with testosterone-fuelled bravado. Vigorous shouts of encouragement, bordering on accusations, were being hurled from the sidelines out to the cluster of oblivious players on the pitch, who were giving their all to the game. Beers were clutched, faces were red, sighs of frustration were expelled. Not for the first or last time, I wondered about this behaviour, as old as time, but today I felt myself bristling at it, wanting to distance myself from what I experienced as a toxic, masculine energy.

Still in this mood, I went to the bar at the end of the game to get a drink for myself and a snack for my son, who was yet to emerge from the changing rooms. There was a small queue of people waiting and I joined them, smiling and nodding to the few that I knew. As my turn approached, a man walked up to the bar, back straight and hand confidently raised to the person serving, in an indication that he would like to place his order. As he opened his mouth, I shifted my position and, politely but loudly stated, 'Ah, I was next,' and smiled. He turned and seemingly noticed me for the first time. 'Oh, yes, absolutely, ladies first!' he shot back in a deep, faux-jovial tone. About to give my order, I shut my mouth, turned to him and firmly asserted, 'No, it's not "Ladies first"… I was in fact next to be served,' and then proceeded to order my drink. My heart was racing in anger, but I managed to keep my voice calm and clear.

As I reflected on this on the way home, there was none of the shame that I often feel when I am outspoken or assertive, conditioned as I am by my childhood experience of being labelled 'precocious' and the social expectation to be mild-mannered and subservient to men, with which all women grow up. I was both proud of myself for speaking up and incensed that we still live in a society that is largely dominated by outdated masculine norms. From this tiny moment, my radar became sensitised, and I began to see injustice, inequality, sexism and misogyny, as well as gendered ageism, in places where I was blind to it before. And I do so still. It exhausts me and it excites me. In her fabulous book about the power of older women, Sharon Blackie shares a quote about menopause from an Indigenous elder, Paula Gunn-Allen, which has started to resonate with me: 'As the bleeding stops, the fire goes within' (Blackie, 2022, p.60).

For me, my midlife transition seems to be about courage and justice as well as a deeper connection with nature and my body. Make no mistake, it is also about my menopause symptoms: insomnia, headaches, exhaustion, brain fog, waves of crushing anxiety and a strong desire to avoid events where I am expected to be sociable. And there is more to come, I am sure. The experience for each of us is different – for our clients and for all those around us in our lives. If we stay curious and open to those experiences, despite their huge discomfort, it may help to ease us in.

One of the dilemmas of working as a psychotherapist is living fully and being authentic in the counselling relationship while also being there, consistently, for our clients. After all, we are not robots, and our shared humanity is a rich seam within the counselling process. According to existential philosophy, the essence of being human is this 'ontological solidarity' with others (Sartre, 1956/2003). Therefore, the work of therapy is to live life together rather than to solve specific problems (Spinelli, 2007). To paraphrase Fritz Perls, co-founder of Gestalt therapy, rather than looking through windows to the client's world when we are practising therapy, we are gazing into a mirror (Perls, 1969). What happens when our ontology, our being in the world, gets in the way of our work? Personal crises, illness, life transitions, responsibilities for our dependants and more can all mean we may need to adapt our practice or ask our clients for some flexibility when scheduling sessions. The work becomes more complex for all counsellors, regardless of gender, as we approach midlife; it can be frustrating, but it can also be empowering.

With specific reference to the menopause, regardless of the increase in media coverage and awareness-raising campaigns in more recent years, there is still considerable stigma and shame associated with it that drives women's experiences underground. Indeed, even in the counselling profession, one that is so heavily dominated by women of middle- to-older age – it has been estimated that 62% of BACP members at any one time could be menopausal (Bodza et al., 2019) – there is a limited narrative about menopause in the literature. Research into therapists' experience of menopause suggests a clear need for a deeper understanding about its effects within psychotherapy, on both a professional and a personal level (Griffiths et al., 2010). This increased awareness and understanding would provide acknowledgement for counsellors and clients of their lived experience, as well as practical and ethical guidance. It is for precisely this reason that I felt compelled to write this book – to inform and encourage psychotherapists, and other psychological and healthcare practitioners, to live with and work with the vibrancy of this midlife maelstrom; to rescue it from stigma, stereotype and victimhood, and acknowledge its primacy both as healing process and experience.

When I embarked on my first counselling training, I was 38 years old. The group was an eclectic mix of a few younger women who were doing it, they said, to help others; one man in his 40s – a supply teacher, as I recall; and a majority of middle-aged or older women who, like me, were changing careers or adding to their skills, and were currently already holding down demanding jobs or roles – carers, nurses, a family lawyer. In our coffee breaks, conversations would often turn to the dilemma of whether you can be a good counsellor if you haven't lived a full life yourself, with all its highs and lows. The implied (and insulting to our younger colleagues) sub-text was that older is better if you are going to be an effective counsellor. And yet, even then, with very little theory, training or experience, I felt uncomfortable with this implicit assumption (as I was with the fact that, through all my training, women were in the majority).

I discussed this with Emmy van Deurzen, the fearless existential psychotherapist, educationalist and philosopher whose writings are a clarion call to take our knocks, face our fears, get back on our feet and learn, learn, learn from adversities. I asked for her views on ageing in our profession. Her answers were that being a therapist channels much of our elder energy; that ageing should be an internal conversation where we are reflective, imaginative and curious about life, rather than an external process. She qualified in her early 20s and was teaching by her mid-20s, and recalls that she often stood out as being 'older than her age' due to innately being this way – an incongruity in a profession that, at the time, during the late 1970s, was dominated by older male theorists and practitioners. 'The truth is I have always longed to be in my 70s and 80s. I was always mature for my age, and I chose to use that and go into this profession, where that maturity or wisdom resonates,' Emmy told me. She said that, throughout much of her career, she has been biding her time until her demographic maturity catches up with her energy and way of being.

As psychologist Sharon Blackie writes, in her vibrant book *Hagitude* (2022): 'Menopause comes knocking at our door… to reclaim the old, potent sense of magic in the everyday, and reclothe it in all the deep, embodied and grounded wisdom we've accrued along the way' (p.60). This makes me reflect on how powerful it can be for a female counsellor to transition into old age and occupy our rightful place as a wise woman, bringing a wealth of rich experience to our work. Indeed, for all counsellors of any age, our life experiences provide a potent resource for our work with others.

One hopeful, bright Monday morning, I blustered my way through the impeccable hallway of my own counsellor's home and into her garden-facing therapy room. Shedding my coat and dumping my mobile phone and bag on the strategically placed side chair, I fell back into an armchair, looked over towards her and smiled. She raised an eyebrow kindly, 'Tea?' she asked. I nodded with a laugh and settled myself, taking a long gulp of water from the glass next to me and considering the scene outside the window as she went into the next room and busied herself with the kettle. Not for the first time while sitting there, I watched a solitary robin bounce happily across the plant pots and finally settle on one, cocking its head at me inquisitively. Behind it was a small pond, edges obscured by paving and ornaments, its glossy surface reflecting tiny clouds and rippling slightly in the breeze. The tall trees that crowned the garden gently swayed in support of the robin's question: 'What's with you today?'

What wasn't with me? As my body surrendered to the chair, I could feel it palpably throbbing with unease. A potent and unrefined cocktail of innocuous thoughts, deep hurt, industrious worry, things to be remembered, sharp sadness and pensive considerations competed for attention. Behind my eyes, tears were pressing, waiting to breach the wall I had hastily thrown up to get through the past few hours of duty and logistics of family life. Irritability, after nights of restless and elusive sleep, was flickering around me like electrical energy on a sultry afternoon, ready to combust at any moment. I felt that if I opened my mouth to speak, I would have no control over what might come out or where this session might go. I felt full of righteousness and mildly ridiculous all at once. Was all this even real, or was it all hormonal nonsense? I almost felt too exhausted to go through the process of finding out. My counsellor, whom I will call Rose, seemed to sense this. As she placed the tea on the side table next to me and took her seat opposite, she breathed deeply: 'No rush,' she told me. 'Perhaps just take a moment to be in the room and "arrive".'

I can't remember exactly what happened or what I said now, of course, but what I remember about almost every session I had with her are the feelings, the physical sensations, the particular dance between Rose and I, and the places of disconnect and connection between us. I feel the moments when I grow or heal, in particular those that happen within counselling, as imprints on my sense of self, and I can conjure them up very easily. I had been working with Rose for several months, curious to experience a new counsellor and keen to come back to my own therapy after a few years' break. It so happened that this coincided with a major event in my family, and this therapeutic space became a welcome vessel for my own pain and grief so that I could help contain that of others. I do feel that the timing was fortuitous and perhaps, as ever, the universe had somehow brought me there, as Rose was able to help me reach a place of acceptance of my own life transition.

Midlife transition, due to its connectedness to ageing and biology, is a deeply embodied experience. As with any embodied experience, such as injury, illness or disability, clients may often notice its effects in their therapist, and the therapeutic process may be impacted. Peers tell me they sometimes forget where they are in the flow of a session or, worse, their client's name. Others struggle to keep their body temperature constant or experience days when they feel so anxious that they question their ability to be of any useful service to their client, or they have to cancel sessions due to sudden, unpredictable headaches. As I've said already, we are called on as counsellors to be steady and constant in our relating to clients and fully present and available to what is being experienced in the room. When the therapist's menopausal symptoms begin to interfere with that, it can cause a crisis, and for some clients, it can stop them coming to therapy entirely (Bodza et al., 2019).

This of course brings up the question of disclosure. Is it in the service of the client for the therapist to disclose any discomfort or symptoms related to menopause? Take as an example what happens when a counsellor is pregnant. This is usually disclosed, as it becomes obvious and there is a need to plan for what happens once the baby arrives, or for any unforeseen problems. If a counsellor has a bad back, a broken leg or any other visible difficulty that needs to be adapted to, this will also be discussed. Why not menopause?

Megan, a counselling colleague and personal friend, is in the throes of her menopause but also has an energy-limiting chronic condition. We talk often about how our shifting lived experience of being in the world impacts our work. Megan has adapted her practice to make space for the symptoms that can overwhelm her. 'I am used to having to be open about my symptoms,' she told me. 'I do this as a natural part of the contracting process. I mention that I have certain symptoms that can flare up from time to time and I negotiate with each client how we will navigate that together. Mostly, I reassure clients that, if I have to cancel a session, I will fit them in as soon as I can. I find it better to talk about this openly, up front, as it gives clients permission not to work with me if this isn't something they want to go through, and it releases me from undue worry.'

Recently, she had endured a run of daily migraines, one of the most vivid of her menopause symptoms, and had been unable to work for a week. When she recommences sessions after having to take a break, she always acknowledges what has happened and allows time for the client to process this with her, she told me. 'And this always brings something new, all grist for the mill!' she said, with a wink.

One client kept telling her that it wasn't her fault and that he knew she wouldn't have cancelled if it hadn't been important. 'After the third or so time of him saying this, I asked him if he was struggling with it perhaps? Saying it was okay but in fact feeling something else? He told me that he trusted me but internally he was battling with his feelings of rejection; he was trying to regulate those two parts of himself as we were talking!'

This was helpful for the client's awareness of their process, but Megan was also conscious of what she might be bringing into the session. There are many layers of experiencing and influence that can happen within one fleeting intersubjective moment, such as this. When a rupture or any relational dynamic happens between the counsellor and a client, each brings to it all of their own lived experience and past experiences, as well as the joint process happening between them in the room. 'As we were talking, I think I noticed that the perfectionist in me was coming forward – the part that doesn't like to fail; the sibling in the shadow of a successful sister; the youngest child in the school year with something to prove. This part of me heard my client's words and, instead of seeing the part of him that was needing reassurance, I felt a criticism, a challenge that I hadn't been good enough.' Megan described how she owned up to these feelings with her client and reminded him about their early discussions about illness and time off. She felt that it helped build another layer of trust between them. 'I felt able to say that my health condition had been worsened by menopause. Disclosing that went against everything I thought I had heard in my training, but it also felt right to say it. It was true. I was being human. I wasn't trying to make excuses, but I wanted to be realistic.'

My own instinct as a humanistic, existential therapist is to work phenomenologically with what is happening between me and the client, as it is happening. Moments when we get something wrong or our fallibility or vulnerability is exposed are not to be skipped over, as they can undoubtedly generate a response from our clients. We must navigate them with care. However, rupture brings the potential for repair and maybe for growth. In a way this is a mirror of our early phase of development where we begin negotiating the realities of psychic differentiation from our caregivers to find our own footing in the world (Stern, 1985). It is the psychological version of taking off the stabilisers when learning to ride a bike – wobbling independently off down the road, with an adult running alongside, a gentle hand in the small of our back to steady and guide us. In the moments where our humanness brings about changes in our practice, I believe that, even if all we do as counsellors is notice the patterns we and our client are being pulled into, as with Megan and her client, there is still the potential for something different and new to happen (Bott & Howard, 2012).

Statistics tell us that 45% of women take time off work due to reduced efficiency during the menopause, 26% due to poor quality of work and 7% due to poor concentration (Newson & Lewis, 2019). Given this, it's inevitable that a considerable number of female counsellors are likely to experience some impact due to their menopause symptoms. Pretending otherwise denies our reality. That bright morning when I arrived at Rose's house, practically overspilling with thoughts and emotions, with everything feeling just too much, one thought rose above the rest: 'I am supposed to have it all together. If I am this chaotic, how is anyone supposed to trust me as a counsellor?' So, that is where I started, with the reassuring cup of tea in my hands.

As I voiced the words, I felt the panic rising in me. I couldn't tell how much sense I was making; the sentences were tumbling out in such a muddle. Rose sat quietly, allowing me space to bring all this forth. She didn't look shocked. I remember not censoring or holding anything back and I feel sure this was possible because she stayed present and took the full force and incoherence of what I was needing to express. Crucially, she didn't interrupt or try to summarise or reassure me. Thinking back now to that session, I feel that what Rose gave me was a safe, cushioned landing for what I was expressing, so that it didn't shatter and disperse but lay there, waiting for me to revisit and scrutinise it as the session unfolded. There were tears – helpless, tired tears, tears of frustration and definitely tears of loss. As my ramblings slowed, I squeezed my eyes closed and pressed my fingers into my temples: 'Aargh, I have no more of an idea how I feel now than I did before I started talking!'

'How did it feel to get some of that out?' Rose asked.

'Good, but it doesn't really get me anywhere,' I replied.

'Where was it you felt you wanted to be?'

'I just want to feel a bit more "together", I suppose. How am I supposed to do my work, coordinate my children's lives, vaguely keep the house and be there for friends and family if I am all over the place?' I smiled and added, quickly, 'And you are now going to ask me what "together" would look like, right?' Counselling a counsellor is always going to be tricky, and I am under no illusion that being my counsellor must have been more than a little frustrating. Rose gently lobbed back my challenge.

'Well, I wasn't, but as you posed such a great question, why don't you answer it…'

'Well, I guess it would look something like you. Here we are in your lovely home; it's calm, you are calm, and it feels safe. I would like to hope my clients feel the same when they are with me.'

'If you lean into what you said about me for a moment, does it feel true?'

'Yes!'

'I am really having to try not to rescue you here,' admitted Rose. 'I confess that I find some things difficult too, and I'm struggling not to list the times I can remember when I have been less than calm in our sessions! I am wondering why I'm trying to rescue you?' She looked thoughtful.

I know that in that session I wanted to believe that everything was awful for me and that I couldn't cope. Constructing Rose as eminently capable and flawless, even when she wasn't (there were definitely times when she lost of her train of thought, scrambled for a word, or requested to change the time of a session, for example) served a purpose for me – a very specific one: it reinforced the idea that I was in crisis by comparison. It kept me within a victim paradigm, isolated and alone in my despair. As we explored this through this session, and others that followed, what I came to realise is that, when things crescendoed for me, usually driven by hormones or lack of sleep, thinking catastrophically gave me a get-out clause. It gave me an excuse, or indeed the energetic push, to press the eject or pause button. Why couldn't I do that anyway? Lack of energy? Lack of self-belief, maybe? What I needed instead, we discovered, was to be my own companion, my own adult with the steadying hand on my back; to track how I was feeling and put in place restorative practices to stop me getting to that point. I needed to regulate myself gently and constantly, which could help me avoid boom and bust.

I started with letting go of the idea that I had to support everyone to the detriment of my own energy. I consulted my GP about my hormone levels and subsequently started on HRT, which, hallelujah, almost immediately helped my sleep. And I gave myself regular breaks and stronger boundaries around when and how I engaged with friends, social events and commitments. This didn't happen overnight, of course; I am fast-forwarding for the sake of the narrative here, but it was a considered progression of steps towards self-regulating self-care.

Above all, counsellors are human. Our sense of self, our lived experience in the moment and the rich tapestries of our lives undoubtedly come into our work, even if not explicitly acknowledged. Supervision and personal therapy are where we consistently observe and calibrate this in service of our clients. Sometimes we get it wrong; we misstep, and when we do it isn't always obvious – at least, not to the client. But it is our responsibility to notice and acknowledge when we are judging someone by our own reality or by our own preconceived beliefs, and to work actively, sensitively and responsively with what emerges from these moments, be it anger, frustration or rejection. And as this often happens on a micro-scale, we do need to stay constantly alert to the possibility.

Alex, a long-term client in her mid-40s, felt secure enough in our therapeutic relationship to call me out directly when this happened in one of our sessions. We were meeting online, which sometimes resulted in us both struggling to feel with our bodies during our sessions, meaning we both tended to stay in our heads, in a thinking, rational place. When working with menopause, I think the body is a very important element, but including it in the process can sometimes be harder to do online. At the time this session took place, I was starting to read more about menopause and becoming curious about my own experience, with the physical symptoms just starting to show. This, I think, meant I was hearing Alex through a filter of my own experience, which clouded my vision from truly seeing hers.

She had been wondering recently if she was in her perimenopause, as she'd noticed some changes to her menstrual cycle and moods. 'I am having a really heavy period at the moment, and I'm washed out, in a lot of pain and kind of angry with my body. Work is so crazy busy at the moment, and I don't have time for this!' she told me, putting her head in her hands. 'I'm so done with all of this biology, literally. Why do we have to go through it?'

I remember thinking that I really understood what she was saying here: that it felt really unfair that, when we are done with our fertility and our periods, we then must live through it getting worse before they stop all together. Why couldn't we just take a tablet and for it to go away? Earlier in our work together, Alex had experienced a late and particularly heavy period – a suspected early miscarriage. I also remember noting that Alex was saying she was angry with her body, and thinking maybe there was more to this; maybe she also felt a loss or a grief? Both these thoughts were about me, or at best about generalisations, fed by the preponderance of women's stories in the media about how awful menopause can be and textbook lists of what a woman (which woman?) might experience emotionally; neither of them was about Alex's reality.

So, when I said, 'Hmmm, is there anything else within the anger? Often when we feel angry it can be a more acceptable emotion that is covering for another that we can't yet name…' Alex did not follow me. 'I'm angry because I am in pain and going through all of this nonsense for what? Nothing good comes from it,' she stated. Then she stopped abruptly and looked at me askance.

I missed the clues, still stuck in the narrative of my own making: 'And what would "good" be for you, I wonder?'

'Absolutely nothing,' Alex said. 'I've never had kids and I genuinely feel okay about that. I am not missing anything… I literally have all the downsides of a part of me that I don't even need.' As she spoke, she raised and lowered her hand to emphasise each part of her reply, her tone reflecting her frustration. This quickly jolted me back into her reality. I paused to allow her words to settle and then, softer and a little unsure now, asked, 'This part that you don't need, where do you locate it?' Alex considered this and said simply, with a dismissive wave of her hand, 'It is not even within my body, it's fictional. I hear other people talk about their biological clock and how their [here she made air quotes with her fingers] "ovaries ache" when they see tiny babies, and I just think, well, bugger off, really. They think that is all being a woman is about. And for me it isn't.'

This vehemence knocked the breath out of me – I had just done the same to her. The counselling space should be a place where people are free of the oppression of 'other people'. These days, menopause is much more around us in the social narrative, and this is helpful, but it is also dangerous. It can become another box to put people in, a filter we can lazily apply in our interactions with others, a label to explain how they feel and behave, and in doing this, we ignore their unique story. We therapists must work harder.

All life experiences are inescapably relational. Freud – and I am paraphrasing wildly here – believed that the first and only dilemma in life following our birth is the fact that, in order to live fully, we must live our lives in relation to others, which creates a series of crises from which we emerge changed, even grown. And the menopause as an experience is also relational: between women and society, between us and our mothers and grandmothers, between versions of ourselves, past present and future, between us and our partners or families and between us and our workplaces and the built environment around us. If we are in counselling, it is undoubtedly through the therapeutic relationship that we can find healing and growth. This relationship has potency because it holds the possibility of creating a new experience for people. It is a space where the counsellor can represent the Other for their client – i.e. the rest of the society or their other relationships – and also a space where, by being offered time to explore their uniqueness, the client is offered the possibility of a different experience (Cooper, 2003; Bott & Howard, 2012). The counselling space should be the antidote to a world that likes to box us in categories, where people are not seen as objects, not labelled, not objectified – a space where we should be able to experience the potentiality of what we are (van Deurzen, 2002).

In counselling, our job is to be aware of stereotypes and work to locate the unique identity of the person before us. The easiest way to do this is to be curious, to ask, to hold the space for their stories and accounts to be told, to be reflective about how we feel in relation to this person, and then to explore this together. As my work with Alex unfolded, this moment of mismatch helped me to press reset on my assumptions. I would love to say that we talked through that difficult moment and resolved it there, within that session, but it wasn't as straightforward as that. I felt I had lost some of her trust, and it had to be regained. Intuitively, over the next few months, I brought my focus and approach sharply into the idiographic, searching for and staying with Alex's unique experience and language, building a picture of her landscape as she saw it and we navigated through it together. And we are still in it together – the long and powerful journey of her self-discovery is ongoing.

It is also important, I believe, for counsellors to consider that, in being honest about how we are in our body, we may give permission for our clients to be the same. We can model being authentic about our own needs and non-judgemental about theirs. My own counsellor made this very easy for me when she was authentic about her own experiences, although I don't think this was a deliberate ploy. In one of our first sessions, she calmly took off her cardigan and asked if I would mind if she opened the window closest to her as she was having a hot flush. She did this completely naturally, and it paved the way for me to notice my own needs and not be embarrassed or ashamed to mention them.

It is important to consider, however, how we might work with someone in therapy who is in the throes of debilitating symptoms. It is no different from how we would approach work with any client who discloses limitations or considerations that may impact the therapy. The quickest route to finding the answer is to ask the expert – the person in front of you. We can collaborate with clients on what they need, both physically and environmentally, 'in the room' and in the relationship. If you are already talking openly about menopause with a client, I believe it is very helpful to ask how they are feeling in their body on that day. This helps the client unearth and negotiate these adaptations in their home and work environments as well. One perimenopausal client I work with experiences crippling periods. These often mean she doesn't feel comfortable attending therapy in person, preferring to stay at home and meet online so that she can manage her needs in terms of pain management and sanitary protection. She doesn't feel safe to leave the house in case she has a debilitating leak of blood.

As I write this, I realise I am struggling to find the right words – might I offend readers if I am too graphic? I notice how the generalised shame about women's biology censors even me.

With any client, our role as a practitioner is to guide them to be curious about their whole self – mind, body, spirit and relationships – in order to find clues to what is going on for them. I find it helpful to ask female clients directly where they are in their menopause journey. I find that some haven't considered it (fewer these days, admittedly, due to the preponderance of media coverage about menopause); some are through it; others are dreading it. I find it helpful, if it feels right in the flow of the therapeutic space, to consider how people of any gender feel about their place in space and time – about their life stage and the meaning it has for them. As author and psychotherapist Stella Duffy bluntly exclaimed when I interviewed her on the topic, 'For women, menopause is a wake-up call to your mortality. It says "Hi, you are dying" right in our faces.' In my experience, men, too, often talk about middle age as the start of the end of life and as if ageing were a deficiency disease. We need to be sensitive when we introduce the idea of ageing and life transitions and in our therapeutic work with it and around it, precisely because there are no givens or constants. However, what we mustn't do is avoid it. There is enough taboo about midlife, enough shame surrounding menopause, without counsellors perpetuating society's discomfort about what is an entirely natural occurrence.

For example, consider a counsellor working with a woman in her 40s who, inexplicably, begins to feel anxious and low in confidence, or a woman who feels her husband doesn't understand her anymore, who feels the distance between them widening week by week. If we don't open the conversation to midlife and menopause and biological changes, we risk missing a large part of her lived experience. It is useful, and indeed ethical, to keep up to date with information about menopause and check with our supervisor what knowledge and resources they might have that can help. Supervision can be a powerful tool for reflecting on our own cultural filters or parts of our clients' experience that we may be closing off.

As a simple remedy to this, at the very least when supporting women and men who are in the 40–60 age range, we should bring their physical experience and views on their life stage into our assessment questions. And then, if we gently bring our focus to their unique embodied and internal experience, our clients may feel seen and more connected to themselves, may recognise where they are and where they might be going as the therapy progresses. We should notice our client's language in relation to their sense of self, their identity, role and place in the world, and explore how this might be shifting and why. Does loss feature in their life, and where? How does it show up? We should notice how we experience our client's embodied self. How do they hold themself? Where do they feel their emotions in their body? We should bring attention to what they might be holding and how they relate to their body. Is this changing, usual, surprising? In this way, the counselling 'room' becomes a place where this significant threshold is named, and the space is actively held for people to encounter their experience of midlife.

Being in my own reflective space in my personal counselling has absolutely allowed me to begin to own my midlife experience. Naming my experiences and being curious about them has helped me make sense and meaning from them: the times when I feel full of rage; when I notice a growing, deepening sadness and panic as my children one by one say goodbye to childhood; when I forget the words to songs I have been singing for years and fear for my cognitive health. Drawing meaning from these has allowed me to set sail across my midlife transition and stay afloat and roughly on course, rather than be tossed around by its unpredictable waves and capsized by its sudden gusts. It has taught me the need to be honest in my own practice: if I forget a word or lose my train of thought, I don't try to cover it up; I voice what is happening, wait patiently for it to return or try to find an alternative. I am not embarrassed or ashamed by it.

So, what else can help? GP and menopause specialist Sam Brown talks to women in her clinic not just about hormone therapy but also about the various lifestyle and social changes that can support them during the menopause. They include good sleep hygiene, reducing alcohol intake, taking regular exercise such as walking, considering gentle, relaxing activities like yoga, and practising any self-care routines that they enjoy. She says that, although there are food supplements that are believed to help with menopause symptoms, simply eating a healthy diet is the best option. She is also a strong advocate for sharing experiences with others – talking to colleagues, friends and family, and being as open as you can about how you feel and the symptoms you are experiencing. It really is good to talk.

'It can feel like a big change. Talking about it is a great way to explore the emotional landscape and to process changes to your body, your relationships, your past and your identity,' Brown told me. She also had some very practical advice about managing your life around menopause symptoms: 'Life can be very busy at this life stage. It can be hard to take notice of which symptoms are happening when, and what the pattern looks like across a month or year. I recommend making a diary of symptoms, so you have a clear picture of what is going on. Then you can plan your week or month ahead, predict what you might need and put in those things first, be it exercise, rest, good food or whatever.'

As I've previously discussed, much of the literature around menopause, and indeed much of this book, focuses on vulnerability. But vulnerability isn't the same as victimhood. By only focusing on deficiency or helplessness, we miss much else in the picture. If we don't allow the prospect of growth and strength to emerge, we may miss the full experience of transition. Nikki Giovanni, American poet, commentator, activist and educator, is widely quoted as saying (Barr, 2007):

A lot of people resist transition and therefore never allow themselves to enjoy who they are. Embrace the change, no matter what it is; once you do, you can learn about the new world you're in and take advantage of it. You still bring to bear all your prior experience, but you are riding on another level. It's completely liberating.

Some of this magic and mystery can be found in connecting with nature or with spirituality, with something bigger and wider than us. This is not unique to women; men in midlife often talk about wanting to find more purpose in order to orientate themselves. In contemplating the meaning and imagery around my own transition in my counselling, I began to conceptualise my growth in the run-up to my 50s as an outward rather than upward process. I can feel myself pulling away from individual exploits and seeking connections around me. It has begun to feel more important to me to hold the space for others to grow, to weave a supportive web for others. I notice that I compare myself less with other people and feel a sense of contentment in seeing others flourish. I absolutely believe that this comes from working on self-acceptance, but I also believe it has evolved out of and is evidenced by my relatively new obsession with swimming in nature. Alone, immersed and floating in the middle of a body of water, I always feel in awe of my surroundings, and I feel part of something much bigger than me, with all my body.

Yasmin is a counsellor in her early 40s with young children and a keen interest in developing her practice into outdoor therapy. She told me that her mother went through menopause early, at 38, shortly after Yasmin was born, so she has always anticipated early menopause for herself too. While she doesn't have strong physical symptoms, she has been noticing some changes. She feels her nervous system is shifting and, to her surprise, finds herself increasingly drawn to the outdoors. She also told me she has become fascinated by other people's stories and wisdom. She told me: 'It's so strange. It's almost like I am drawn to feel like I am in a tribe. I want to hear stories of what has gone before and learn from the experience of others. I have just joined a women's outdoor group near me. I was on a training course for wild therapy recently and we were encouraged to go and sit near a tree of our choice and spend some time with it. My younger self would have giggled at that! But I found it so moving, I leant into it, felt its strength, and found myself wanting to connect to its ancient energy. It was like an instinct from my body, not from my mind.'

She went on to tell me that she has always dreaded her menopause; her mother's stories had been full of discomfort and crisis and accounts from mainstream media had only reinforced that for her. What she hadn't expected was to feel strength from connecting to nature. 'She is, after all, a natural mother to all of us,' she explained to me. Yasmin said she feels sure she will emerge as something more than she is today, and that her sense of self will be richer once her transition has happened. She hopes the changes she is making to her counselling approach and practice will support this.

As counsellors we sit alongside our clients in their uncertainty and vulnerability; we give these feelings room and permission to emerge so clients may find growth within the space we offer. Arguably, we can, and often do, afford the same generosity to ourselves. Perhaps the shift that is needed is one that is outside of us. Claire Arnold-Baker, counselling psychologist, existential psychotherapist and a specialist on the psychology of motherhood, told me: 'We have lost track of what's important. In society at the moment everything is growthful and productive, there is no room for a slowing down or softening. Things that aren't about money or work are not valued. We have lost sense of what is important, how we are living is important.'

By embracing, adapting to, and living courageously within our humanness, with all its experiences, we can surely model a different way of being for others.

Chapter 6
Putting on a show

Midway upon the journey of our life
I found myself within a forest dark,
For the straightforward pathway had been lost.
Dante Alighieri, *The Divine Comedy, Vol. 1: Inferno.*
(c.1321/2009, Canto I, lines 1–3)

I'm always interested to observe my first impressions of how someone inhabits the space around them when they first arrive in my counselling room. Some enter tentatively, almost soundlessly, waiting to be invited in and asked to take a seat, full of politeness and reticence. Some dance about me in the hall space that leads to the room, uncertain of where to go but wanting to be in some kind of control of the situation. This new client, Andrew, walked confidently through the hallway, straight past my arm pointing him towards the counselling room, sat down in the chair without discussion about which one he should take and seized its arms decisively. His body seemed to occupy more space than its contours needed. With his set jaw and twitching muscles, he was larger than life. Although not physically tall, his presence was palpable. The air felt charged. I found myself taking a deep breath to clear my mind and ground my body. I smiled.

'It's good to meet you and have you here. Where would you like to start?

Andrew had emailed me only a few days earlier, asking to meet me and enquiring about my availability. Our exchanges were brief and to the point; in two emails, we had a session booked in. He asked for my bank details in advance and had paid the session fee an hour before arriving. This isn't unusual with male clients, I have noticed; order and process seem to provide a guardrail into the therapy room. As this first session eased itself off the starting blocks and into its first moments, I tried to centre myself in the here and now and focus on the essence of what Andrew was bringing, to avoid slipping into making any assumptions about him based on his compelling and energetic physical presence.

'Right,' Andrew began, releasing his hands to form loose fists that rested more lightly on the chair arms: 'It was my wife who suggested I come. I've reached what I suppose you could call a crossroads, and probably a list of other awful metaphors, and I need some help getting through it.' He stopped as abruptly as he started.

'I see,' I replied (which I didn't, yet) and continued, 'Can you tell me more about that?' Those first two sentences of his were so evocative of a stereotype of 'man in late 40s' that I felt no closer to really knowing what Andrew wanted from me.

'Hmmm… I'm not really sure what you want to know but let me give you a few facts, I suppose.'

I noticed Andrew's language here; it felt a little bit as if he was talking to a doctor, giving information so I could give him a diagnosis. This became an ongoing feature of our early months together, one that we would work with and around many times. At this point, however, I wasn't sure if this impression had come from his language or from my own filters. I concentrated on listening in hard and tried to hold very lightly any picture I was unwittingly building of him. We had, after all, only just begun.

'So, I am a bricklayer now. I work part time and when it suits me, really. I used to work in TV and film production, cameras mostly; I loved using my hands and I loved the industry, but it broke me. Years on the road, being away from home, late nights, drinking – you name it, we did it. I left my job, did lots of other jobs, nothing felt the same really. Bricklaying keeps me physical and gets me out of my head. You know, those thoughts you'd just rather not have? But recently I've had chronic pain in my joints and

I'm finding work hard; I'm going to be 55 pretty soon, and that is the downward slide into old age, right? When I'm off work, that's a lot of time just sitting around and I'm no good at that. So, I don't really know what to do next.'

I opened my mouth to say something, but he continued, waving his hand towards me. 'Hence, the crossroads.'

I smiled gently in response. 'And this sitting around and thinking, and being at a crossroads, how is this for you?'

'Ah,' he paused a little to think, 'It's kind of annoying.'

I still felt I couldn't yet properly grasp his experience. I felt quite disconnected not just from what he was saying but from him too, truth to tell.

'Let me see if I can understand that more deeply. What does annoying feel like...? For you, I mean.' Here I placed my hand involuntarily on my heart, encouraging him to connect with what he was saying.

'Yeah, like I just want it to go away,' Andrew said.

'It's uncomfortable?' I suggested.

'Oh, it's more than that; it's bloody painful, physically and mentally, I suppose.'

'Ah, so this experience is painful on many levels, and so no wonder you want to try to move beyond it.'

'Yup,' Andrew affirmed.

'And you used the phrase "crossroads", so I am taking that to mean that you don't yet have the answer within yourself as to which direction to go in.'

'Uhuh,' he agreed, with a blink.

Unapologetically, much of the focus of this book has been on women's experiences and the menopause. It started out with that as its sole focus, to serve as an antidote to the marginalisation of women's experience that persists within contemporary workplaces, society, medical research and culture. I aimed to spark more awareness-raising and training within the psychotherapy community in working with clients in menopause. However, the book grew to encompass midlife and to look more widely at the human experience of this major transition across the genders. Midlife is, I realised, no less commonly overlooked or presented with a strongly negative bias as the threshold of the downward path to death for us all.

In this chapter, I will look at men's experiences of midlife and the andropause and explore the meaning of midlife for them. The topic undoubtedly deserves a book in its own right: all the data sources I visited when researching this book agree that men in middle age are much more at risk than any other population group of dying by suicide, much greater than women are, and that this current middle-aged generation (Generation X) is at higher risk than any other (Dattani et al., 2023). In England and Wales, death by suicide is three times more common in men, with the highest rate among men aged 50–54, and this heightened risk is exponentially rising (ONS, 2022a). That said, the mental health statistics unanimously show that the groups most likely to experience mental health distress are in fact people who identify as LGBTQIA+ (2–3 times more likely), black people and women aged 16–24 (Mind, 2023). From this we can deduce, perhaps, that middle-aged men are dying by suicide in high numbers but not seeking help for mental health problems. As practitioners, this should interest us; what stops this demographic from accessing support and what is going on that might be causing such distress that they end their own lives?

Let's first deal head on with the topic of the male menopause, formally known as the andropause. Every woman will experience the menopause at some point in her life and with some kind of symptom (if only the cessation of her monthly periods). Menopause is a biological process that occurs in all women when their ovaries stop producing eggs. This is typically marked by several physical and emotional changes, including hot flushes, night sweats, mood swings and a decline in hormone levels. Men do not have a similar process as their hormone levels do not typically decline in the same way as menopausal women's. While testosterone levels decline as part of the ageing process from the mid-40s onwards, they do not do so as drastically and uniformly, and mostly with far less symptomatology. However, men may well experience other physical and emotional changes, such as an increase in body fat, a decline in muscle mass, and a decrease in libido and self-confidence (NHS, 2023). While these changes form part of the normal ageing process, they are nevertheless disorientating to experience.

Seismic life changes may arguably be navigated with more proficiency by women due to the amount of undulating physical and psychological change through their lives, such as the onset of puberty, menstruation, becoming a mother or not, or experiencing baby loss, and then our subsequent menopause. A man's life, by contrast, is socially and biologically constructed as more linear, in an embodied way at least. It is often, and more usually, a response to a succession of expectations of productivity handed down from their parents (often with a disproportionate influence of the father) and by society about what 'male' means: career, marriage, children, home, financial security and so on. Once these have been achieved, or become less easy to fulfil, a crisis may well indeed occur. Ageing is one of the most obvious prompts to begin to fully consider our death, whether we do so consciously or not, and this can create feelings of meaninglessness and searching. So, midlife may cause something of a shock to many men, existentially as well as physically, and it might be the first time they have experienced a change so powerful.

Consider Willy Loman, the central character in Arthur Miller's definitive play about midlife, *Death of a Salesman* (1945/2015). He is a salesman and a family man, struggling to find success and meaning through hard times and midlife, realising that he has not lived up to his own expectations or the considerable weight of expectation of his family. 'He's a man… riding on a smile and the shoeshine. And when they start not smiling back, that's an earthquake,' explains Miller (1949/2015, p.111). Loman eventually declines into paranoia and becomes locked into thinking only about the past – the archetype of later life in developmental psychologists Erikson and Erikson's model of life stages – the point where people can end up descending into stagnation or despair (1998).

David, an accountant in his mid-40s, who came to see me for help with his own earthquake, told me he felt he was stuck in a pressure box: 'There is this unwritten rule we are all following, you know: provide for your family, have an uninterrupted linear career, peak as high as you can, do what the company wants you to do.' He told me that he had never before had an inflection point, a moment when significant change occurs, or any natural breaks or direction changes to his career, and that what he was now experiencing had been creating feelings of panic and anxiety. 'And it just gets worse the older you get; the stakes of stepping off that well-worn path just get higher and higher, I felt like I had no freedom.' David told me he had a strong relationship with his wife and was able to identify what was happening, and she had encouraged him to seek help for how he was feeling. He also told me that this vulnerability he felt made him more empathetic with others and that it had taken him into new avenues at work, particularly around mentoring and championing others in the workplace. This is what Erikson called generativity (Erikson & Erikson, 1998) – nurturing things that will outlast us, fostering positive changes that benefit others.

It holds true in my client work and in the research that many men experience a broad wide range of physical, emotional and psychological changes during midlife. These can include changes in physical health and appearance, shifts in career and personal relationships, and an increased awareness of their own mortality. One man I spoke to, a successful operations manager who had enjoyed a straightforward career trajectory, experienced a physical and mental crisis as he approached his midlife. This came out of the blue, prompted by a change of role at work, and it directly challenged his sense of self, which he had previously thought of as independent, resilient and capable. It also prompted a re-triggering of a long-term health condition that took away his ability to box, his beloved sport, which in turn impacted his confidence and his relationship with his wife. 'Usually, I punch my way into solutions, but I didn't have the resources to do that, and it scared me,' he told me.

Yet, as with women, the experiences of men in midlife can vary greatly and are influenced by a wide range of factors, including individual differences, cultural background and life circumstances. Some experience a sense of crisis during this time; others experience it as a period of personal growth and renewal, one in which they are able to step off the productivity line and engage with emotions and activities they might never have paused to contemplate previously in their driven, goal-oriented lives. Holding this awareness is helpful when working with male clients.

As I previously mentioned, it was the Canadian psychoanalyst Elliott Jaques who, in 1965, famously coined the now ubiquitous term 'midlife crisis' to describe the psychological emergency that he believed many people experience in the middle years of their lives (Jackson, 2020). According to Jaques, this crisis is caused by a person's realisation that they are no longer young and that their mortality is approaching. This can lead to feelings of despair, a sense of loss, and a reassessment of their lives, prompting some to make drastic changes to find meaning and fulfilment. If midlife in women is seen as being mostly synonymous with menopause, midlife in men is generally regarded as a period of such 'crises'. The term is widely used and understood, but as with any aspect of human experience, we must be careful not to generalise, especially in counselling; generalisations can exclude and isolate people who do not fit the expected norm and prevent us attending to the person's unique lived experience. Midlife (and notably men's midlife) is so rife with stereotypes that we must be hypervigilant not to be influenced by them.

Andrew mentioned the stereotype in his first couple of sentences. I could sense from his narrative that he had concluded he was having his own midlife crisis, and I felt it might be important to locate what was happening for him in something more specific, more personal.

'Can you tell me more about this pain? Do you feel it now?' I asked.

'It's there all the time, but yes I can feel it now,' he replied.

'And this is the physical pain you can feel?'

'Yes,' Andrew replied.

'I wonder if you can describe it to me, so I can understand it with you?' I asked.

Andrew told me he had pain in his hands, knees and elbow joints mostly; that the pain was often sharp and enduring and made him stiffen up if he stayed still too long. It was worse when he had been exerting himself. 'Right now, it's about a 5 or 6; it's grumbling, but not enough for me not to be able to think straight.' He pressed his hands together, massaging them, as he spoke.

I was curious what his relationship had been to physical pain in his life thus far and asked him about it. 'Ha!' he replied, 'Pain is weakness leaving the body, right?' I raised a questioning eyebrow: where had he learned that? 'That's what they tell you in military training,' Andrew continued. He explained that he had left school at 16; he'd been quite bright and done quite well in his O-level exams, but his father and mother were both teachers and this made him adamant not to follow in their footsteps. Always having been good at sport at school – 'It gave me a role in school, I was good at it, and it got me accepted' – the logical route for him seemed to be the army.

He went through gruelling basic training and spent a few years in the Armed Forces, then left when he married. 'Training in the army is all about putting your body and mind under more and more pressure and pain, and those of us that survive that onslaught get to stay. What a prize!' he concluded, bitterly.

'Okay, so your tolerance for and acceptance of pain was part of who you were, who you still are?' I asked.

'100% yes,' he said. 'I've always been able to blast through it. I kind of think of it as my superpower.'

I was conscious that Andrew had talked about his current predicament in terms of both physical and mental pain. I reminded him of that and asked him what mental pain felt like.

'Argh! I just feel useless for one. Never, ever have I felt useless. That's torture to me. We've recently moved into a new house. This isn't new for us; we get bored easily and we have moved a few times. We always move ourselves as it's cheaper, and between me and friends and family, we usually get the job done – hire a van, you know, and it's done right. We are literally sitting around with furniture in the wrong places and boxes still to unpack at the moment and it's killing me that I can't just whizz around and get it done!'

I noticed something about the words he was using. 'Hmmm. Your language today has a lot of energy and movement in it. I wonder if you notice that too?' I wanted to highlight it as it might be important.

'Huh, like what?' Andrew asked, head on one side, questioningly.

'You said "blast" and "whizz" and talked of "superpowers", and they seem to be very, well, energetic,' I replied. At this Andrew stopped and let the idea sink in. 'Yeah, that's kind of who I am,' he said.

I trod carefully here: 'But I wonder if you are *just* that? Because at the moment you are not able to be that way, is there any other part of you that you notice?'

At this, I observed a tiny change in Andrew's demeanour. His shoulders softened a little, his gaze, which had been direct and held mine, drifted off slightly. It was subtle but it was there. 'I'm not really sure what you mean…' he started to reply.

'No, I didn't really make myself clear, it was a bit vague!' I apologised. 'What I suppose I mean is that you have come here today, and I can see, and hear, that you are a capable and strong man. And you've said that when you are forced to be still and rest because of pain, it's mentally very hard for you. I get the impression that there are parts of you that are just as valuable, but you aren't as familiar with or accepting of them.'

I felt pretty sure that, even on the rephrase, I was losing him. I laughed at myself and tried a more direct approach: 'Tell me what I'm not yet seeing, what might you not want to bring here yet.'

'Errrr,' he winced, 'vulnerability?' I stayed quiet. 'Weakness, maybe,' he added.

'These are things that you hide?' I checked.

'Yes, they don't give me anything and I don't like to think of myself having them.'

'Because...'

'Because then I get hurt, or I hurt others. Bad things happen.'

A counsellor's role is to explore the unique reality of our client's worlds, listen out for clues, challenge constructs of their own or others' making, and encourage them, with us as their companion, to bravely face up to that which is painful, holding them back or in crisis. We simultaneously represent 'the other' who experiences our client's way of being in the world, and we can also be, as Ernesto Spinelli calls it, 'the exception to the rule' (2006): we provide a different experience. I find the challenge of this quiet subversion to be very rewarding, both for me in my role and for my clients. We can broadly hold ideas and philosophies as a framework, but the only truth is the one being revealed by the client, with all its potential, as the counselling process unfolds. From the first moment of meeting Andrew, I could feel the force of his strength, and I also felt compelled to see what was being obscured by it. Maybe part of him was even asking me to see it. I hoped that he would learn to see and value whatever he was hiding, too, in time.

Where we were getting to, in this first session, was an understanding of how Andrew's sense of self was entering a crisis because his ageing body was getting in the way of him maintaining and protecting his self-image as a strong and productive person. However, this crisis was also showing up in his relationship. Andrew's wife, Karen, had changed her career in recent years, he told me. She'd left her job in the corporate environment and embarked on a gradual journey of self-discovery, having followed her dream of training to be an acupuncturist. Conversations between them at home had shifted from the mundane and practical topics typical of a busy family with growing (now adult) children, to a more intimate searching for a closeness as a couple. This shift had prompted Andrew to reflect more on himself and, perhaps, protect himself. As we worked through this, it became apparent that profound relational trauma, well-hidden and firmly tucked away, was beginning to surface. Within their relationship, the shifting of one person was colliding with and influencing the shifting of the other, which is quite usual, particularly at a time of shared life transitions.

Andrew had been talking about a recent argument they'd had over one of their grown-up children, who had been visiting that weekend. 'I left the house. I could feel myself closing down and I needed to get away and be on my own. I'm not proud of it, but I stormed out, took the car and went to the beach where I sometimes walk the dogs.'

'You needed to be away from Karen in that moment?'

'From her, from everyone. It was too much. It's like… well, it was like I couldn't get any air.'

'Can you remember what it felt like, in your body?' I asked.

Here Andrew paused and cocked his head. 'Like a pressure in my chest.' I invited him to place his hand on his chest to connect with that memory a bit deeper, and then mirrored him.

'It feels like I am claustrophobic. It's panicky, fluttering and painful,' he said

'And as you recall that now, do you notice anything else?' I asked.

'Stupid?' Andrew threw the word away, seeming to joke.

'Aside from a judgement,' I smiled, 'anything else.'

Andrew told me he felt childish, young even. 'So let me reflect this back,' I said. We were both still holding our hands to our chest. 'The argument made you feel claustrophobic, and instinctively that you needed to get away, and this feeling of running away or panicking brings a feeling of being young, and of being "stupid". Your word not mine,' I emphasised for clarity.

'Hmmm, yes.'

'And as I say that, what do you make of it,' I invited. 'You look lost in thought!'

'I don't know, but two memories pop up. One is from when I am young; I wasn't at school at the time, so maybe aged three or four, when I was scared in the night and crying out. No one ever came. I just can remember the darkness of the room and looking at the light under the door, willing someone to come. And the other is from much later, when I went into basic training for the army. I took the train there and my parents didn't see me off or really say goodbye. I remember turning up and seeing the other recruits having emotional farewells with family and I arrived alone.' He sat back a little after saying this, eyes lowered.

'And as you bring these memories here, now, what comes?' I asked gently.

'I just don't know how to do real closeness; I don't trust it. When Karen starts at me, for all the right reasons, about what I am thinking or feeling, or how we are as a couple, I can feel myself retreating, like I am going down a tunnel away from her right to the very end.'

'What is it like in this tunnel, I wonder?'

'It's kind of safe. I can still see her but there is a distance between us.'

As in *Death of a Salesman*, the realisation that all is not as it was, that one's own self and the relationship we have with the world has shifted on its axis, can be experienced as an earthquake – in Feiler's words (2021), a 'lifequake' – one that rocks the foundations of our identity. As our work had been progressing, Andrew was starting to open up to a new experience – one of physical vulnerability – and this coincided with an increasing emotional vulnerability in his relationship with his wife, which he welcomed on one level but found hard to tolerate due to his past.

Another man I spoke with in my research, an actor with a prominent public persona whom I will call Michael, noticed a change when he turned 45. Years of touring and being away from home had left his relationships on rocky ground. At the same time, he noticed his passion was waning for the high-octane environment he worked in and the attention it gave him. The public accolades also seemed to be dropping off, with some reviews implying that he was no longer in his prime. He told me: 'It was all adrenalin and no realness. I think I started to change and wanted more of a connection with people, and, cheesy as it sounds, I also needed more of a purpose. It all began to feel empty. I just wanted to be in the same place and have more of a quiet life, maybe find a new relationship.'

If we are in an intimate relationship, we may find we are coexisting with a partner who may also be going through their own lifequake, almost certainly at a different pace and with different meanings for them to ours. For Michael, now entering his second marriage, this brought a crushing realness into his life. He described how painful it was for him watching his wife going through chronic menopause symptoms: 'I feel helpless but we just make sure we talk a lot and always give each other space if it is a tough time. It's like a see-saw really: when one is down the other leans to help and vice versa. We have none of that innocent naivety of a young, new couple.'

For men, counselling can be a place that provides holding and stability at this time of uncertainty, and a place to explore a sense of vulnerability that they may not have experienced or may have been unable to allow themselves to experience for a long time. It may well trigger feelings or patterns from earlier in their lives. A strong, trusting therapeutic bond and the sense of deep acceptance that we hope our clients experience with us helps them to maintain a sense of cohesion and self-worth while they confront and review the fundamental features of their identity and relationships. Holding a safe space for that also supports clients to allow their vulnerability to surface within other relationships over time. I felt I wanted to reinforce for Andrew that finding a way to establish safety for himself within his relationship would be a source of strength, particularly given some of the early relational trauma that we had begun to explore in recent months. I said as much to him now: 'Using your image of a tunnel might be a helpful way for you to stay with Karen in the room while keeping yourself safe, but also when you feel yourself wanting to run or go into the tunnel, that's a good early sign for you to indicate to her that you need to pull back. So, as you move forward in deepening your relationship, this self-awareness and shared narrative could be helpful.'

Andrew thought this a good idea and we spent a little time going through how he could do that.

But there was something more, something about his relationship with himself, that needed to find safety too. In my practice with clients in midlife and beyond, and in particular with male clients but not exclusively, I have noticed that it can be powerful to identify the different parts of the self that were developed across the life span and to support a healing and gentle dialogue between them. Our internalised younger, current and older selves can often support, encourage and challenge each other in a way that is more meaningful and lasting than a therapist/client dialogue. As changing and declining hormones are often playing their part, it is helpful to be curious and alive to how patterns or narratives from teenage years might show up. For example, for someone who was self-conscious or bullied at school, or who came into puberty later than most, there may be a seam of shame that hasn't yet been acknowledged but is making its presence known in thoughts, feelings and behaviours. Many men who come into counselling express a strong connection between self-worth and their embodied sense of being in the world. Bringing this all into awareness and understanding helps our clients to better navigate their internal world at this time of transition.

Andrew and I met weekly for some three years. As time went on and our therapeutic relationship built, we began to encounter more and more this young, pre-teen self, who had in fact experienced sustained relational trauma. He had previously been quite dismissive or judgemental about this part of him, seeing his young self as weak for not fighting back against what our conversations revealed to be a torrent of emotional neglect and physical and psychological punishment. Slowly, very gradually, we began to develop a closeness with and compassion for this young Andrew. His current adult (and now midlife) self, who was nurturing his self-worth and beginning to relate confidently with other people, began metaphorically to put his arm around his younger self. This image, which he described to me in a session one day, came to him while out on a walk. 'I was thinking about the stories and memories I had been sharing here with you and I suddenly had a sense of how shocking and awful they must sound when you hear them,' he explained.

'You heard them as if you were someone else listening to them,' I echoed back to him.

'Yes, and I suddenly felt sad. He didn't deserve any of it! It's funny, I used to feel so much shame about what happened but now I kind of feel angry for him.'

'For *him*?' I quietly repeated. I felt suddenly breathless, not wanting to make any move that might interrupt what I hoped was emerging.

'Well, no, for *me*,' he laughed, drily.

'Can you repeat what you said, but connect it with you?' I asked.

'Yeah. I didn't bloody deserve it!'

'And if your younger self were here now, and you had your arm around him, can he hear that?'

'Yes, I think so,' Andrew replied.

'How is he reacting? What is he feeling?' I encouraged him to say more.

'Relieved, I suppose. Like he can just let go of thinking that it was his fault.'

'It wasn't his fault that it happened?' I repeated.

'No, it wasn't his fault – it wasn't my fault – and it's going to be okay.' Andrew was now warming to his theme. 'I will make him okay as I am stronger now, emotionally. That's why I have my arm around him.'

Andrew went quiet, pensive and inward-focused. I left him in a silence for a bit. When he brought his gaze back to me, it was direct, emphatic even.

'And how are you feeling?' I asked.

'Good,' he nodded. 'Good… and slightly more whole, and a bit overwhelmed!' He laughed. 'I am going to need to ruminate on this, I think.'

Rarely do we get a neat and happy ending in therapy. It is always my hope that we have started something powerful enough for it to have the momentum to go on to create all sorts of changes in the lives of those of our clients who choose to do the work for themselves. This image, these moments together, became the force that catapulted Andrew into lasting healing and change. He was able to accept that he was both strong *and* vulnerable and to use each of these sensibilities in combination in his life, whatever it threw up for him. It was a privilege to journey with him, sense this deep shift and see how it scaffolded his midlife journey and onwards into this different-looking future.

The midlife period of our lives is often a time of introspection and self-evaluation, as we begin to reflect on our lives and consider accomplishments and failures, goals and aspirations, relationships and sense of purpose. Almost certainly, men are less used to such seismic shifts of self and tend less towards self-reflection than women overall, but many men will feel the tug of these new sentiments at some point. These are all big feelings and will undoubtedly impact our lives and our work.

It isn't rare to hear of people, like Michael, feeling they want to move into work with more meaning. Michael found it much harder to 'put on an act' as he approached midlife – something within him was searching for authentic connection after years of superficial performance. Through a chance meeting with an old industry connection, Michael moved into producing independent investigative TV documentaries, unearthing and exposing injustices. When we spoke, he was almost perplexed by this turn of events, but told me he was grateful every day for a steady job, a happy relationship and what he called a 'blissfully unremarkable life'.

The process of self-reflection can be both positive and negative: it can propel us inwards towards stasis or forwards towards growth. Some men feel a sense of crisis or loss and grapple with the realisation that their career is over, their lifetime of productivity is finished; they are literally redundant in the workplace, and mortality is approaching. Others may experience it as a time of personal growth and renewal, as they make changes in their lives and seek new directions, challenges and experiences. This was the case for both Andrew and Michael. In therapy, our best and only task is to be alongside people, stay curious, and facilitate a safe, non-judgemental space for these emergent experiences to surface and to be explored.

When Andrew and I finished our work together it was his decision, and we planned it over several months. In our final session, I reflected on the directness and bravado I had experienced when he came into the counselling room for our first session. I wondered what he made of that now. 'I felt so weird coming into this room and talking about myself, it took everything I had to come that first time and not leave as soon as you looked at me across the room!' he laughed. 'I think I was probably putting on some sort of armour to stop you from getting in and seeing me. Fat lot of good that did me!'

He was interested, he said, in how I experienced him now. We laughed that the tables had turned – that sounded like a very 'me' thing to say. 'Well, Andrew, I see you in all your glory. All the parts, all the ages and all the work you have done.' We sat for a little moment in silence. Andrew swallowed visibly, and I thought I saw tears in his eyes. Then he laughed and blinked them away. 'Oh dammit. I definitely didn't want to cry today but I feel like I'm going to let myself, actually. Consider it a parting gift!' he said, hands outstretched, his body open and relaxed, in such contrast to that first day.

In the Eriksons' theory, if we are successful in being generative during our midlife stage, if we are creative in exploring who we are, we find integrity. This post-narcissistic view of our self allows us to find our place in the world and an acceptance of our life as 'the only one meant to be' (Erikson & Erickson, 1998, p.87). I often question developmental theory, as it was largely constructed around men and only uses male pronouns, but this makes it especially fitting when considering male experiences. As an alternative viewpoint, the prominent female commentator on life transitions Gail Sheehy (1998) sees midlife as an opportunity for men to be free of old ways of being: 'An old shell can be sloughed off and space made for a yeasty, multi-dimensional "new self" to grow' (p.85), she writes. I think this beautifully describes the hope and potential that the midlife transition offers men. Instead of shedding his former self, I like to think that Andrew got to know all his selves and brought them powerfully together to live in concert – in particular, his adult 'now' self and his younger self who was in emotional pain. This image will never leave me. I think of him often, and hope he is going well.

Chapter 7
The sum of all the parts

The whole is *other* than the sum of its parts.
Kurt Koffka, *Principles of Gestalt Psychology* (1935/2014,
p.176)

I don't ask for your pity, but just for your understanding – not
even that – no. Just for some recognition of me in you, and the
enemy, time, in us all.
Tennessee Williams, *Sweet Bird of Youth* (1959/2009)

'Do you know much about hormones and stuff?'

I had been working online with Cate, a woman in her mid-40s,
for more than three years, helping her through a bold and stressful
career move that had brought some 'old wounds', as she called them,
to the surface. Cate had been hoping that coming to therapy would
help sustain her resilience and fortitude as she embarked on a high-
stakes job that she hoped would be her last big move before coming
out of corporate life and following her dream of training to become
a music therapist, working with children. Her partner, Rona, was 15
years older than her and had taken early retirement.

What a strange question for me, I thought. On the screen, I could
see her pen poised over her pad and an open, inquisitive expression
on her face. Behind her was the unmistakeable, asymmetric
background of a loft conversion, and windows showing a late

afternoon grey sky gathering over high-rise buildings. To her right was a large bookcase of carefully colour-coordinated books. Cate was resourceful, analytical, a scientist by training. Why was she asking me something she could research for herself, probably a lot more thoroughly? Where was this going?

'I know a little,' I ventured. 'I am wondering what it is you need to know?'

'Yuh, well, I guess I am curious about what's happening to me at the moment. I am angry a lot, and I mean a *lot*, and my patience with my team, and with Rona, is so short. Nothing seems to measure up or be right at all. And I kind of hate that.'

'You hate that nothing is right?'

'No, I hate being like this,' she quickly corrected me, with a slight frown. 'I don't like myself when I am like this,' and she pointed downwards. We both laughed. I had mistaken her question, and she was irritated.

'Ah, like that?'

'Yes, exactly!' she replied.

This initial conversation triggered a series of sessions across many months where we began to explore Cate's experience of the confluence of hormonal changes (her periods had been increasingly difficult) and her rapidly shifting attitude towards work, which had always previously been in lockstep with her sense of identity. It was a journey that we both stumbled through, in truth. Cate had experienced a linear life, not without its challenges but always moving forward, following a strongly structured plan. Even our counselling modelled this to a certain extent: she came weekly without fail, for many years, always on the same day and at the same time. The counselling process was far from plain sailing for us, and as we navigated it we learnt together how the dominant heterosexual, white, middle-class narrative of midlife tugs against the otherwise natural flow of the experience of those whose lives do not fit within its constricting margins.

On average, my private practice clientele over the years has been around 70% female, 80% heterosexual, 95% white and 0% non-binary or transgender. Of course, this lack of diversity is influenced by my own identity (I am cisgender, female, heterosexual and white), the demographics of where I work from, and how I present myself in my promotional materials and advertising. Some people will not actively seek me out as I don't specifically have the expertise, experience or credibility that fits with their experience. I also have a disproportionate number of clients over the age of 75 years, who in general have a different way of engaging with counsellors. This means the numbers of people from minority communities coming to me for help are still fewer than they might be otherwise: culturally, among Black, Asian and other seniors from racialised minorities, counselling is less likely to be regarded as a useful, or necessary, source of support.

I understand why my practice is not diverse, but it makes me uncomfortable nevertheless, and I am committed to trying to widen my reach. Psychotherapist Humera Quddoos, blogging for the UKCP on its website about being questioned on her experience as a Black therapist, beautifully captures the essence of therapy as an 'effort to understand deeply, to invite honest sharing, to mirror and meet the other in the ground of their being, as they define it' (2003), and this is also my genuine intent: to meet people in their lived experience. Counselling, for me, is all about major life transitions. I believe that how we approach and process them will be informed not only by our origins and how we identify ourselves but also by how we experience being in the world with others and how we fit or don't fit within society's dominant paradigms.

We can agree that ageing and midlife are getting much more coverage than ever before, and that this is largely a positive phenomenon. However, this welcome higher profile in popular culture is problematic in that, once a topic gathers momentum, it begins to solidify into a homogenous form. Even before the menopause started to receive the amount of coverage it has today, most women anticipated that the ending of their reproductive years would occur at some point in their midlife. Most men may find themselves searching for their story within the several dominant tropes, ranging from being wise counsel, financially independent, faded, outdated and grey or seeking recreation in some extreme, risk-taking way. Our awareness of this is dependent on the culture, the environment and the century or decade in which we are situated. In recent history at least, women have learned to expect, maybe even fear, the climacteric (as it was traditionally, academically known), the 'change' (in colloquial Westernised language) or, as it is rather wonderfully described in China, the 'second spring'. In tribal cultures, older women look forward to the end of their labour-intense, child-rearing years, and take their place as elders and carers with pride. In Western and Westernised cultures, we anticipate a time when, as writer Sam Baker jokes in her book *The Shift*, we 'stop caring about the shape of [our] jeans and start wafting contentedly along beaches in wide-legged linen trousers, sensible sandals and floppy hats or become the plate-smashing heroine of the Menopausal Woman' (2020, p.3). Euphemisms aside, wherever we are in the world, there is a certain level of expectation of what lies in wait that orientates us. What happens when we don't find ourselves represented by the dominant narrative, or worse, we don't find ourselves represented within the support structures or services around us? How does that change our lived experience? We all, but most especially those of us supporting others, must work hard to deconstruct the received narrative – to find all of the parts within it, all the experiences, all the colour, all the textures. It is the sum of all its parts.

There are pivotal moments in client work that I remember in technicolour, like highlighted passages in a page of text: insights and learning – sometimes painful – to squirrel away and return to. I had one such moment in my work with Cate and it always serves as a reminder to me not to make assumptions, and to check my filter regularly. I'd allowed a mental stereotype of women in midlife, formed while I was reading and researching the topic, to dominate my worldview – it happened momentarily, but it was an important moment.

Cate had always had troublesome hormone cycles; they put her into depressive, dark states and were physically debilitating. As she aged, Cate's difficulties with her cycle – extreme, what she called 'psychotic' episodes of rage and painful cramping – had morphed into difficulties in perimenopause, such as this irritability and intermittent, unpredictable and heavy blood flow, which she felt could be a harbinger for the end of her cycle. She had been prescribed HRT, which she found helpful in quelling her symptoms and evening out her mood so that she could continue to function. It gave her more predictability over her cycle and her emotions than she had ever experienced before.

This particular day, we were discussing the meaning of this for her, and I had in my mind the idea that menopause carries a degree of loss for women, that she might be grieving for her fertile years.

'I'm wondering how this is for you, the end of your cycle, the start of a different phase of your life?' I said.

'Well,' she replied crossly, 'I literally never needed my periods anyway, they have always plagued me and made me unwell, I can't wait for this to be over and for them to be gone!'

I remember feeling a jolt, like I had bumped into an unexpected object in the dark. It was so obvious, but I'd allowed myself to lose focus on her lived experience and drift into generalisations. As she said, the perimenopause heralded for her a welcome release from a fertility that she hadn't wanted or needed and that just got in the way of what she did want to do.

'And that feels… releasing maybe?' I conjectured, more carefully.

'It's about time really! I'm kind of enjoying it,' she replied.

Cate's childhood, while mostly happy, was not straightforward. She was the result of an early and unplanned pregnancy in the lives of her parents; her two siblings arrived much later, the first when she was 10 and the second two years later. Her parents worked long hours through her early childhood, building their careers and trying to gain financial stability. As a result, she remembers feeling overlooked, lonely and, when her siblings came along, very left out and never quite part of the family. This sense of not belonging led her to travel widely and she felt strongly that she didn't want to have children – a decision that her partner, Rona, whom she met in her mid-30s, shared. Rona, too, had never wanted children.

We hadn't given much time to this in our sessions over the many years we'd been working together. Cate didn't see it as a dilemma that needed resolving; it was simply a part of her life. Most of our focus was on her work, her identity, her resilience and her relationship. I remember, as she began to be perimenopausal and started hormone therapy, how much lighter her energy and language became when talking about life choices and family relationships. I mentioned this one day and Cate mused on it for a while, before replying: 'Well… for years I've had to explain myself to my friends and family and kind of wait in line. You know, we were the ones with more flexibility so we had to kind of go last in the priority needs stakes, and now it's like the playing field has levelled – we aren't "the ones without kids" who can be more available, more flexible about arrangements. I feel more able to say "No, that doesn't work for me" because there isn't this implicit expectation that we are more flexible, more available because we don't have kids. Because now it isn't just a lifestyle choice – we can't, and we are in a different life stage.'

A received and common conception of midlife is that it is a stage when those of us with children grieve the end of our children's childhoods and the start of their independence – the 'empty nest syndrome', as it's often called. They are leaving home, and their parents are waking up in a totally new landscape – free to travel, to do what they please, when they please, and also face to face with the realisation that, for now at least, there are just the two of them in their relationship. It's a completely different experience, of course, for those who are childless, or child-free. It is important to be clear about the difference between the two – between those who are unable to have children or whose child/children have not survived into adulthood (childless) and those who have chosen not to have children (child-free). How a person without children will feel about the end of their fertility and child-rearing years will depend greatly on which of these groups they belong in. The trend for people to choose not to have children is reportedly on the rise (Shpancer, 2019), and their reasons range from concerns about global overpopulation to protecting their career or preferring financial freedom.

Whatever the reason, when a woman who does not have children enters the menopause, with its very stark message that her fertility has ended, she (and her partner) may have very varied reactions, depending on their circumstances. Heterosexually active women may be relieved to no longer have to consider contraception; those for whom child-freedom was a conscious choice may experience regret over their decision or feel resentment towards a life partner whose decision it was; some, like Cate, will just be glad that the whole messy, expensive business of monthly menstruation is over.

Claire Arnold-Baker is a counselling psychologist and existential psychotherapist specialising in working with mothers. Her research has revealed that matrescence (the developmental transition into motherhood, a term first used in 1973 by anthropologist Dana Raphael) is an existential crisis that causes disruption across all dimensions of life: our individual experience, social experience, physical experience and spiritual experience. I discussed this with her when I interviewed her when researching this book. Claire explained: 'Nowhere are we stable or firm. We are unsure of our place in the world as it has radically changed. We are confronted with existence in its rawest form. We are acutely aware of our own mortality and the reality of existence and holding responsibility for someone else. Our relationship with our partner, if we have one, must be renegotiated and we have to, if you like, crash our values and purpose together.' In many ways, when women reach menopause, many of these elements come back into play. Cate's experience, and that of many others, highlights how much we, as a society, idealise motherhood and hold onto an archetype of the perfect mother. There is little acknowledgement of the childless and child-free woman; she is an irrelevance, arguably 'unnatural' in the case of those who have actively chosen this.

It is worth considering what impact this has. How might such women experience the end of their reproductive years? On the surface, the transition could be seen to be easier. Certainly, for one woman I spoke to during my research who had never been able to conceive due to an illness in adolescence, the loss of the potential to have children was a non-event. 'I've already grieved this, 20 years ago, and I am not seen as a mother, so I don't have anything to "undo" and there was nothing for me to miss when it was gone,' she told me. But for others, menopause may revive that grieving process. This could be the case for women who have experienced miscarriage or the perinatal death of a baby. Speaking from my own experience, when my baby died before it was born, there was unspeakable pain, but there was also the hope that I could still have another child. For me, my continued fertility offered the potential for this. Now my fertility is disappearing, I find myself, 17 years later, revisiting my loss and needing to probe it and resolve it again.

I discussed this with writer and existential therapist Stella Duffy. She told me: 'There is a death of our previous bodily version of ourselves. Whether we become mothers or can't or don't, menopause is a wake-up call to our mortality. I genuinely believe that in our culture death is so terrifying and so unspoken about that when menopause shows up and says "Hi, you are dying – your body is changing", we therefore feel anxious. What's wonderful about it is that, out of those ashes, we can grow again.' I reflected deeply after this conversation and it helped me see that acknowledging to ourselves and in our work that each major life transition has an intrinsic link to our biology and our fertility, and hence to life and death, can help us to find a route through these transitions that is deeply authentic and personal.

So, what if we are not 'in the parenthood gang' when we approach the age of our midlife? Around 1% of women in the UK experience the menopause before 40 years of age; this is known as premature menopause. It is also known more brutally in the medical literature as premature ovarian insufficiency (POI) – a term that already constructs it as a deficiency disease. Another 5% of women in the UK experience the start of their menopause transition naturally before the age of 45 years – the age that is the general norm. In a few exceptional cases, women may become menopausal naturally in their 30s, or even younger (NHS Inform, 2023b). These are menopause transitions that fall outside of the linear, usual timeline, meaning that when these women reach midlife in terms of years of age, their experience can be very different.

Research from the 1960s and 1970s, which still holds currency today, identified that socially structured ways of thinking about the changes that occur from birth to death, and their significance, orientate us and help us organise our lives (Neugarten & Hagestad 1976). It also revealed that normatively constructed age frameworks are further reinforced by consensus and social control. Today, we have come a long way from the rigidity of the second half of the 20th century, when there were stronger expectations of the normal timelines of developmental events. Changing demographics, shifting and more diverse social norms, as well as the rise of individualism in the past few decades mean there is now a degree of flexibility in our expectations of what should happen when. Yet, arguably, the power of social consensus is again becoming reinforced, thanks to the pervasion of social media. What is it like to experience 'out-of-time' life events, especially when the normativity of others' timelines is made so visible to us? We counsellors need to be alert to the responses it might provoke, which could be anything from indifference to disorientation, from grief to liberation.

Some life events present themselves abruptly and suddenly without any warning; not all are anticipated. If a woman has to have a hysterectomy to remove her ovaries, she will experience the menopause immediately after the operation, regardless of her age. This procedure abruptly induces menopause by eliminating the primary source of oestrogen and progesterone in a woman's body. (It is also possible to enter menopause without removal of the ovaries, as they may have reduced function due to the trauma of surgery.) According to the most recent estimate I could source, some 4,000 women in the UK undergo such surgical procedures per year (Sturgis, 2016). Although these data are well out of date, I couldn't find any more recent, reliable statistics. In the US it is estimated that 36,000 women a year under the age of 45 undergo a surgical menopause (Salimi et al., 2019).

It is statistically more likely that women will be aged between 40 and 50 when undergoing a hysterectomy (NHS Inform, 2023b; Johns Hopkins Medicine, 2023), so they may well have been thinking about and preparing for natural menopause, if not already starting to transition, when they had surgery. But the sudden loss of ovarian hormones through surgical menopause generally results in more drastic symptoms than does natural menopause, with more debilitating health outcomes later in life (Namazi et al., 2019). The oestrogen deficiency resulting from surgical menopause is associated with an increased risk of cardiovascular disease, stroke, osteoporosis, cognitive changes and urogenital atrophy – and all these are more prevalent in premenopausal women who undergo induced menopause (The North American Menopause Society, 2023). While statistically far from the norm, entering the menopause 'out-of-time' and in this unpredictable, sometimes extremely shocking way can have considerable impact on a woman's mental health and sense of identity and mortality over her remaining lifetime. This is in addition to a raft of physical ramifications that can be life-changing and are difficult to distinguish or separate from the effects of major surgery.

Medically induced menopause following breast cancer also falls outside of the natural or accepted order of things. This has received some attention in the research in recent years as female survivors of breast cancer are proving to be at increased risk of suicide (Carreira et al., 2018). As many as one in seven women will experience breast cancer, and there is a clear link between breast cancer treatment and menopause, as oestrogen levels are affected in both. This means menopause may be one of the many impacts that breast cancer survivors must endure. As menopause expert Dr Louise Newson explains (Newson et al., 2022):

> The many individuals who survive breast cancer may suffer with after-effects of treatment and develop severe menopausal symptoms which can have a big impact on their quality of life after breast cancer. (p.1)

The raised risk of suicide among those who have received breast cancer treatment is greatest among younger survivors. Reasons cited for this include a shifting outlook about life and death, psychological conditions such as depression, and both cognitive and sexual difficulties caused by the cancer treatment and/or changing hormone levels in the body (Carreira et al., 2018). Louise Newson highlights how lonely the experience of breast cancer treatment can be for those going through it. She urges women to talk about how they are feeling and seek help through counselling if it becomes overwhelming (Newson et al., 2022).

The term 'midlife' becomes problematic for those who experience midlife transition outside the parameters of what is usually regarded as midlife. What if we reach that transition earlier, either naturally or due to illnesses or other life events? Midlife, by definition, makes assumptions about our age and life stage. And for women, most of the narrative revolves around menopause. If we don't conform to this biological and statistical norm, it can be isolating. We humans like to put people into categories and boxes – it gives us certainty, the security of predictability, and helps us make meaning of our lives. However, it is at best tiring and frustrating to have to explain why it is different for you when you don't conform to these norms; at worst it creates a sense of abnormality, exclusion, difference and otherness. We have a responsibility as therapists to be mindful of this possibility and stay constantly vigilant that we do not erase the experience of the person before us. With Cate, our longstanding relationship and the fact that the topic hadn't arisen before made me complacent. I assumed, when I should have stayed open to what she was telling me.

While I was researching for this book, I interviewed a man in his early 40s who described how he came through his own 'crisis' in his late 30s, following the deaths of both his father and his father's father at a time when he was about to become a father himself. He told me that the prevailing narratives in the media, in literature and in imagery had no resonance for him as he looked towards what is generally understood as 'midlife'. 'What I went through in my 30s felt like the end of my younger life and I started thinking about my new role in the world as the top of our family tree. I wondered about my death, my place in the world, and I sometimes felt suicidal,' he told me. He went on to say he felt weakened and de-powered at that time and somehow impotent, with little hope for the future. It was only now, as he neared his mid-40s, that he had regained hope, he told me. He felt optimistic, changed, vibrant and finally living within his purpose. Any suggestion that he might be facing a midlife crisis would have been met with incomprehension, as bearing no resemblance to the richness of this stage in his life.

I also spoke with Virginia, now in her late 50s, who had been post-menopausal since her mid-30s, following cancer treatment. When her cancer and subsequent menopause hit her, she and her wife were trying for a baby. 'I went through six months of chemo, but the drugs put me in menopause within an hour. I'd been prepared for this, in a brief chat with my doctors, but it was still a shock. Even more of a shock was my infertility. Still now, none of the menopause literature focuses on post-cancer or infertility, which angered me at the time.'

For Virginia, her midlife transition was marked by the greying and whitening of her hair, which she celebrated ('It's glorious, look how cool it is!'), by launching into a third career, rich with potential and new beginnings, and the start of a new decade. She was post-menopausal before her midlife showed up, and our discussions about how midlife is represented for women prompted some eye-rolling. A self-defined queer woman, she described to me how she was used to feeling outside the dominant narrative, so this dissonance was not a shock to her. 'We need to get beyond the cis-female, white, hetero-dominant stereotypes for menopause in particular. It's time we did better. We are missing whole swathes of experiences that matter,' she told me. She then went on to politely but firmly point out that I was perpetuating that particular problem in writing about midlife and menopause, as I am also cis-female, white and heterosexual – a point that I readily acknowledged. Her advice to me? 'Go and find out what the other narratives are, and once you see them and you know them, you'd better make sure you represent them.'

Martin Buber, the Austrian philosopher best known for his philosophy of dialogue and arguably one of the godparents of existential thought, saw the problems of human existence as being what happens in the intersubjective space between people (1923/2023), rather than solely within them; therefore, this is where, he argued, the healing can also occur. He believed that there is a pliability or possibility of self when we interact with others. Likewise, psychoanalytic theorist Jacques Lacan's writings propose that the reflection of ourselves as a whole self by others helps us resolve the anxious experience of fragmentation as new-borns, and that this pattern continues throughout our life (1980). Therapy can be a place where people can experience being seen without judgement by someone who can listen and respond to their unique experiences. We sometimes shy away from checking if something genuinely resonates with or negates an individual's experience. Crucially, therapy should provide a space where the individual can be acknowledged for all that they distinctively are and what they feel. The therapist is in a position to act as a counterpoint to the labelling, othering and normative expectations that a person may experience in their close relationships and within society. In my opinion, this is what makes us social activists.

Being 15 years older, Cate's partner Rona had already gone through her midlife transition. Cate told me that having Rona's experience as a reference point did help her; specifically, it signposted what might come, heightening her curiosity and awareness, even though their experiences were very different. When two women in a relationship go through the menopause together, the effects may be compounded – both the good and the challenging. One woman told me it was both incredibly helpful and frustratingly farcical: 'It is a rollercoaster. There seems to never be a time when one of us isn't in the throes of something. But then at least we can both empathise with each other!' Overall, queer menopause can be complex, and here I am using queer to encompass those identifying as LGBTQIA+ – non-binary and trans, as well as those in same-sex relationships (Glyde, 2023). Disturbingly, due to the predominant heteronormative Western medical model, many queer people experience, at best, a lack of understanding, and at worst, blatant discrimination in the healthcare system and in mental healthcare. As writer and psychologist Tania Glyde reports, menopausal clients frequently face multiple discrimination when accessing therapy and healthcare services: acephobia (prejudice against asexuals), ageism, biphobia, homophobia, misogyny and transphobia. This can lead to them feeling isolated and alone, perpetuating mental health problems (Glyde, 2023).

As a white, straight, middle-class woman, I struggled to connect with people in the queer community when researching this book. People were cautious, checking my credentials and the reasons for my questions with much greater diligence than I encountered with cisgender heterosexual interviewees, who may not have experienced, and had less reason to fear, misrepresentation and its consequences. One person I spoke to told me bluntly that it wasn't personal but I had to understand that I represent the very system within which many queer people have experienced everything from incremental micro-aggressions to outright pathologisation. Why, they asked, would people trust and want to talk to me? Recently, in a conversation on inclusion with a queer autism expert and lobbyist, I was brought up short, but not unkindly, when he said: 'I know you mean well but so much damage is done by ill-informed, well-meaning people like you.' Are we as therapists at risk of being exactly that: well-meaning but ill-informed? We have to be better at this, and I include myself in that 'we'. Never are differences most evident than when our lives and selves are subjected to the stress-testing of major life transitions.

I took my misstep with Cate to supervision, of course. I was curious to explore the extent to which my insensitivity to her uniqueness was caused by my own world view. I wondered what else I was missing. The answer to this question revealed itself when her irritation reappeared in a later session. Cate and Rona had recently started hiking as a way of getting Cate away from her desk more and making new friends (she worked remotely and spent most of her time at home, starting early on international calls and often finishing late in the evening). Sometimes, she said, on a rainy or cold day, she would come home from a hike and have a bath and a cup of tea.

'You smiled when you told me about the bath,' I noted.

'Hmmm,' she consented in reply.

'Because? What did it mean for you as you recalled it then?'

I had in mind that fresh air, exercise, baths and other practices like yoga help not only menopausal women but any person going through upheaval and when under stress.

Cate didn't follow me. 'Er, it was a *bath*,' she emphasised, looking me in the eye.

'I guess I wondered if it felt good to be treating yourself…'

'Well yes I suppose so, but really, it was just a bath…'

As we explored this dissonant moment, Cate told me how frustrated she was by what she called the 'pink movement'. 'There seems to be nothing in the media narrative on middle-aged women apart from outright fear and horror on one hand and positive, pink-branded, empowerment on the other. There is no room for nuance.'

'And you situate yourself in the nuance,' I stated.

'Yes, exactly!' She paused, thinking. 'In some ways I feel more "male", you know. I am pushing with my work, my identity is connected to that very closely, and I am pushing for retirement next. I don't dwell on my menopause, as you know. It's clearly happening but it's under control and I am looking forward to when it's done. So, you know, I can't see myself in any of this.'

'And then I just did the same thing, didn't I?'

'Huh?' she replied, not getting the reference.

'Well, I was "pink branding" your bath. Your bath that was, simply, a bath.'

'Ha, yes.'

The idea that menopause can be a benign, even positive experience is not mainstream. For Virginia, the cancer survivor, for example, her menopause formed part of her recovery process – it didn't leave her reeling. She rode it out, as she had the many other physical traumas and tough experiences life had thrown at her. Having grown up in poverty and with violence, having had a near-fatal car accident in her early 20s from which it took her months to recover, having experienced miscarriage in her early 30s and then breast cancer in her mid-30s, she didn't experience the menopause as an embodied shock. She told me that many of the stories and viewpoints on menopause in the public realm are from women for whom this is the first time their body has endured physical or existential hardship.

The research into the relationship of menopausal symptoms to social determinants of health in fact shows that the experience of menopause is influenced heavily by cultural norms, social factors and personal knowledge about menopause (Schoenaker et al., 2014; Williams & Clark, 2000). One of the main divergences is that women who work experience less severe symptoms than those who don't have a job. Another is that women with active lifestyles and whose diets do not include masses of processed foods tend to fare better in menopause than those with less healthy lifestyles. Support systems and education about the menopause can greatly impact a woman's experience, as can our genetic make-up. Some studies suggest that women of African, Hispanic and Asian descent experience fewer hot flashes than do women of European descent (Namazi et al., 2019. Other research has found that, for the majority of women, the menopause is a 'relatively neutral' event, and that women living in Western countries report more symptoms than those from non-Western cultures (Hunter & Rendall, 2007). One thing is for sure, until the body of literature and overriding narrative move beyond white, straight, middle-class, Western viewpoints that overwhelmingly speak to notions of 'victims' and 'survivors', a large population of women will feel under-represented and unseen.

As counsellors, we can hold space for people to narrate and find meaning in their own experience, which in turn requires that this space has capacity to contain a myriad individual experiences. The power of our midlife transition lies in the meaning we make of it for ourselves. Many commentators have noted the scarcity of meaningful, positive cultural templates that focus on possibility and opportunity (Birmingham, 2021). We can help by encouraging people to be intentional and reflective about what is happening for them and to write their own story about it. Research shows that this can increase the possibility of positive psychological outcomes. In *Counter-Clockwise*, her book that takes issue with positive popular psychology and uses hard research to report the real influence of mindset on health and wellbeing, Ellen Langer presents evidence that our beliefs about ageing can impact the symptoms and experience we have during these life transitions (Langer, 2010). She finds that people may be able to enhance their wellbeing by cultivating personal, positive beliefs grounded in individual meaning, and by challenging negative stereotypes. She highlights the importance of maintaining a sense of control and autonomy in the face of ageing. Therapy is one such place that offers us the possibility of exploring how we want to frame our own experience, which gives us some control over it. For those who are experiencing 'off-time' or non-typical transitions, this is undoubtedly even more important.

How do we make sure we don't inadvertently silence those we work with, or harm them with generalisations? In my work, I find that supervision allows me to notice if I am objectifying people. I can tell it is happening when I make broad statements or begin to lean too heavily on theory. These two things naturally take me further from the uniqueness of the person in front of me. One very effective way of noticing this is to listen out for generalisations that sneak into the narrative in supervision sessions. Look out for 'pink washing'. When I'm writing up my notes and in supervision, I try to pause to reflect and check if I am filtering anything; to notice what I am not saying, or how I am talking about something, as well as name any assumptions I am making. We can, and should, momentarily and irrevocably provide our clients with an experience that is different to the usual and thereby create the possibility for change for them. In this way, therapy becomes an emancipatory act on both an intimate and a social level – a small but focused and powerful rebellion.

Chapter 8
The top of the tree

Because when an elder dies a library is burned, and throughout
the world, libraries are ablaze.
Elizabeth Lindsey, *Curating Humanity's Heritage*
(TEDWomen, 2010)

Therefore myself is that one only thing
I hold to use or waste, to keep or give;
My sole possession every day I live,
And still mine own despite Time's winnowing.
Christina Rosetti, '*The Thread of Life*' (1895/2008)

Experiencing the ageing and death of our parents, whenever it
happens, brings into stark relief our own mortality. This is because,
even if we hadn't considered it until now, generationally speaking,
we are very likely to be the next to die. And, practically speaking,
whether we embrace it or accept it ourselves, we have slowly
ascended the branches of the family tree and we are now at the top.
This can be a heavy burden, particularly if deeply ingrained family
dynamics or childhood patterns have not been resolved – pain,
conflict and hurt can carry itself from one generation to another
if not reconciled or processed (Samuel, 2022). We are the elders in
waiting, often unconsciously or reluctantly, at least at first, and this
is a heady experience. For Sylvia, a woman in her late 50s, this reality

emerged abruptly and surprisingly out of the fog of grief for her best friend, and it caught her off guard.

The confluence of our own busy, meaningful midlife years with the decline of our parents is a growing phenomenon. This is due to the unique combination of two factors: increased longevity and longer working years. In the UK, average life expectancy has increased by five years from 75 to 80 since 1990, consistent with the trend across Europe as a whole (The World Bank, 2020). If you are 65 years old now, you can (on average) expect to live another 20 years (ONS, 2022b). In the US overall, it is slightly lower, at 77 years. More of us will be working through our 60s and beyond, in unprecedented numbers, due to falling birthrate trends and reduced migration. Older workers now account for nearly one third (32.6%) of the UK workforce; there are more than 1.2 million workers over the age of 65 and this figure is predicted to increase (CIPD, 2022). This means younger people will soon be outnumbered by older people in the workforce. The impacts of the Covid pandemic have changed the landscape somewhat (Centre for Ageing Better, 2022). However, the data reflect the reality for many people in their midlife years, who are experiencing a 'pinch point' where our own midlives are dominated by not just the search for purpose in our own life, questions about the directions of our continued career path and keeping a sense of self in a shifting world, but also by the considerable pressure of worrying about and caring for our elderly parents or other family members.

Sylvia had come to counselling in the raw and early days following the death of her closest and most loved friend, Nicky. They'd known each other since primary school, and their friendship had endured and transcended distance, the occasional fallout and, between them, three marriages and seven children. Nicky, Sylvia told me in our early sessions, was the one constant in her life, and was more like family to her than her own family. In the months leading up to Nicky's death from cancer, Sylvia had held everything together, visiting her daily after work, but when Nicky died, Sylvia felt like everything was falling apart. Her confidence at work had disappeared, she told me, and family relationships were strained; the tenancy agreement for her home had come up for renewal and the landlord now wanted to sell. She felt anchorless and adrift.

When we first met, Sylvia struck me as softly spoken, quick to smile and eager to accommodate and fit in with others. I had an impression that she was someone who tried not to occupy too much space. I noticed she arrived promptly every week, always checked the clock so as not to overrun (even when I joked that it was my responsibility) and tended to apologise profusely for any interruption to the flow of our conversation, such as a cough or a sneeze. She spent the first few sessions pouring out her grief, anger and sadness at the death of her best friend, her 'rock'. The sessions were a container for the volume of these emotions that came forth. Halfway through one of these early sessions, Sylvia was talking about a family dinner that had been arranged for her birthday. She was dreading it. In fact, she didn't want to go. 'Everyone will be there – my sisters, their kids, my lot, the grandchildren and my mum, obviously, and they will all be expecting me to be grateful and happy and I just don't know if I have the energy to pull that off. I just want to hide,' she said. There was so much to unpack in that sentence, but one thing in particular stood out to me. I wanted to see what Sylvia had heard, though, so I echoed her last few words: 'You just want to hide from all of that.' At this, Sylvia crossed her legs and folded her arms, bringing the scarf she was wearing closer around her body, as though acting out the protective instinct about which she was talking.

'Yep, I honestly hate all of that at the best of times, but it will be so loud and so, well you know, *dramatic* and over the top,' she continued, and rolled her eyes.

'What happens to you when things are dramatic, I wonder?'

Sylvia batted this off with a sweep of one hand, almost as if I hadn't spoken. 'Do you know what, it's not actually the drama of it, now you say that; it's the fact that still, after all this time, and even when I am bloody well in the depths of grief and holding onto my life barely by a thread, I will turn up to *my* birthday meal and that woman will somehow still make it all about her and still make me feel like I have done something wrong or somehow ruined it.' She sighed and tightened her grip on her body further. 'Urrrrrghhhh!' she exhaled, her frustration palpable, and then, predictably, opened her hands out to me: 'So sorry for swearing by the way.'

I smiled by way of reassurance and, raising an eyebrow, gently asked: 'And by "that woman", you mean…'

'My mother, of course.' I stayed silent, sensing there was more.

'Even in her 80s and with COPD and all her health troubles, she is still as able as ever to ruin a night, or your life, with her resentment.'

'Ah,' I replied.

'She's – what would you call it in your official language? – a narcissist or something? She could make anything be about her. She would find a way for something to be your fault even if you weren't there and had nothing to do with it.' Sylvia paused in thought: 'Quite a talent, right?'

I noticed that Sylvia had slipped from using the term 'me' to 'you' or 'your', and I wondered what was making her distance herself from what she was describing. In my experience, this functions as either protection from or avoidance of something, and usually we are not conscious it is happening. I mentioned this to Sylvia, and that her body language had shifted into a closed posture too, and asked her what she felt made her do that. She was perplexed. 'Did I really?' she asked and seemed to cast her mind back over the last few minutes. 'I don't really know,' she shook her head. 'Sorry, I'm not used to thinking through things like this, I don't really know what to say!' She fumbled with her hands and scarf, self-conscious now. I apologised, feeling that I had been quite clumsy or abrupt.

I reset: 'It might be easier for me to say how I experienced what just happened. I felt you were here in a physical sense, but I felt you retreat from me a little, as it were, and your language seemed more like you were talking about someone else.'

'Hmmm,' she pondered this for a while. 'Yeah, well, my mum terrifies me. I was probably reacting to that. You can't be off your guard with her. You can't be vulnerable. It all goes wrong,' and here she threw her hands up in frustration. 'I mean "I" can't be rid of her. I did it again, didn't I?' I nodded assent. 'You know, I really thought at least in here I would be free of her, and it took, what, three weeks for her to get in and steal all the attention. Even here, for Christ's sake!'

Clients come into the room and demonstrate to us how they live their lives in every interaction, however small. If we are receptive to noticing it, counsellors are a reflection of the outside world, and we also experience how our client lives within theirs. Being the mirror for this can support their growth in the long term, as it can help reveal what is there so we can then unpack it. What Sylvia and I had experienced together in those moments was how invasive and pervasive her mother's presence was in her life, even in the counselling room. I believe that, if we counsellors are alive and alert to the patterns we and our client are being pulled into, there is the potential for something different and new to happen for them in the long run. Journalist, writer and podcaster Sam Baker exultantly writes in her book on midlife that this is a time for women to make 'the shift from having your narrative laid out for you by society – husband, house, babies, then what? – to becoming storyless. Or as I prefer, story free' (2020, p.4) We can use the microcosm of our relationship to create a catalyst for self-reflection and, ultimately, a rewriting of their story.

We undoubtedly gave Sylvia's mother ample space in our conversations. She overshadowed most of Sylvia's life, but we committed to each other that we would allow this to happen in a way that served Sylvia. This was different to how Sylvia experienced every other intrusion by her mother. She had never been able, she told me, to talk to her mum without feeling she had been judged or reprimanded, and as a result she had never felt able to stand up for herself. By allowing Sylvia to decide how and when she brought her relationship to her mum into the therapeutic space, and checking out if she was comfortable with that, we were starting to give her some practice at establishing those boundaries.

The mother-daughter relationship can be incredibly powerful to explore with female clients, at any time of their lives, as it situates women not only within their gendered generational history but also within their unique, gendered sociocultural context. It can unlock awareness and create the potential for women to transcend what they have inherited. According to psychotherapist and mother-daughter relationship expert Rosjke Hasseldine (2020):

> We see how life events, restrictive gender roles, unrealised career goals, and the expectation that women should sacrifice their needs in their caregiving role all shape how mothers and daughters view themselves and each other and how they communicate.

To get to the roots of this for Sylvia, and to free her from the story that was holding her captive, we needed to go further back, but only when the time was right.

We had been talking one day about Sylvia's views of herself as a mother, as one of her five (now adult) children had been criticising how long it had been taking for her to deal with her grief. They'd had an argument recently and she brought this to one of our sessions. I noticed she was critical of herself as a mother in the way she talked about herself, but there was also something else – a frustration that, after all the years of looking after her children, they didn't seem able to be compassionate and caring for her at this time when she was feeling particularly vulnerable. 'That's just not how families should be. I had hoped mine wouldn't be like that, but it seems it is,' she finished, with a shrug.

'Can you tell me a little about your family of origin? I've realised we haven't talked too much about it, but it might be helpful so we can understand what family represents to you,' I suggested. Then I added, 'Only if it feels comfortable' – remembering that we had made an agreement that she would set the boundaries for herself.

Sylvia was half Italian, half English, the latter being on her father's side. Her mother had come to England as a child, aged 9 or 10, with her family, in the wake of the Second World War. Sylvia remembered her maternal grandmother as forbiddingly strict, but seemingly in awe and under the spell of her husband, Sylvia's maternal grandfather, who worked long hours at a shipbuilding yard. Her mother was the youngest of an extensive set of siblings. 'She was at the bottom of the pile. She fought her way, often with fisticuffs, she said, to get any say among her older siblings. She was the last to have the bathwater on a Sunday night, apparently, and boy doesn't she always go on about it!' Sylvia told me.

Her mother had left home at 16 and trained to be a nurse, coming to London from the south coast and meeting her husband, Sylvia's father, a trainee postmaster. They married and went on to have four children, all girls, in quick succession, and then, finally, after a pause, Sylvia. They lived in a tight-knit, largely Catholic community in south-west London, with Sylvia's mother giving up her job to raise the girls, which she did according to traditional Catholic principles. From the minute Sylvia and her four sisters began to grow into adulthood, their mother's resentment seeped into every aspect of their relationship with her, Sylvia said. She became highly critical and embittered, and created every opportunity she could to bring the family attention onto herself. Invariably, Sylvia told me, she would be ill at someone's wedding, or angry when a grandchild was born and she hadn't been given warning the birth was imminent. She never talked about her own feelings, except to blame them on others.

'What is like to tell that story of your parents and family to me?' I asked Sylvia.

'It has made me realise what a big family we are, and how we never really talk about family stuff any more, if at all, actually. I realise how many gaps there are in the family history too,' Sylvia said, 'But mostly it has made me realise that my mum was the smallest of the small in her family.'

'Hmmm, what do you notice about that particularly?'

'Well, she is the top of the tree now, isn't she. She commands us all,' Sylvia replied, her voice dropping into a tone of faux authority.

'She commands you?'

'Well, no, she bullies us, I reckon,' Sylvia said, sourly.

'Has telling this story given you any insight into her?' Again I noticed that Sylvia crossed her arms and pursed her lips a little. We both spotted it at the same time. 'Ah, you don't want to think of her with tenderness at all?' I checked.

'She doesn't really ever talk about feelings; she normally just acts like she feels something and waits until someone notices. So, it is weird to try and imagine what she might be feeling, if you see what I mean...'.

'I do,' I reassured her. 'If you think of yourself as that little girl, moved here from Italy, fighting her way to get heard inside a big family, with a mother who was strict, what do you think you might feel?'

'Erm... I think I would feel like no one understood me? I would probably look for ways to be loved?... Yeah, I think she would want just to be loved.' Sylvia looked lost in thought, and I felt tears prick my eyes. We were near to something. I, certainly, felt a lot of compassion for this little girl we had conjured into existence. Sylvia looked at me and put her head to one side. Her hand absentmindedly rose to her heart from her lap. 'When I said those words then, I felt like I was talking about myself.' 'Yes,' I breathed, 'I felt something quite powerful then too.'

Sylvia came into counselling at the age of 55. She had been divorced twice and had five children, now aged 18 to 37, and three young grandchildren. She worked full time at a GP practice, where she had been a receptionist for 18 years. She had experienced intense menopausal symptoms a few years previously. They had crept up on her without her realising as she was going through her divorce at the time and thought her incessant tears, sleeplessness and anxiety were solely related to that. Then, when she started on HRT and was beginning to feel more like herself again, Nicky had received her cancer diagnosis.

Sylvia's experience is not so rare; many people find midlife to be a time of intense change, when their responsibilities are greatest: home, job, family, ageing parents. It is at this time, more than ever, that our relationships and support networks become vital, as well as our connection to community. As psychotherapist and author Julia Samuel writes in her book about families, relationships are vital to our health and happiness, and we often overlook the impact of our families on our lives. 'The quality of our lives depends on the quality of our relationships', she writes (2002, p.4). However, Samuel also points out the essential truth that our ability to sustain relationships with others is dependent on a strong relationship with ourself (Samuel, 2022).

While Sylvia had identified an intergenerational experience of being silenced and emotionally neglected, which can be a common theme between mothers and daughters (Hasseldine, 2020), there was something more at play here, something that was uniquely to do with her sense of self. In the months we had been meeting each other, Sylvia had noticed something strange had been happening at work: the pace and volume of work had increased and her usual warm and patient style, which had served her so well up until now, was attracting criticism from her managers. Sylvia usually came to me straight from work, and one day she arrived visibly shaken and flustered.

I took in a breath to centre us. 'Where would you like to start today?' I asked and waited for her to start.

Sylvia held her hands out to me. 'Look at me, I am literally shaking,' she said, breathlessly. 'I feel so anxious,' she explained, wringing her hands together as if to stop them shaking. 'I'm just getting everything wrong. We have a new system to use, and I find it confusing sometimes. Why can't I just be like everyone else? It feels like it's easy for them, but I just can't get it.' As she wasn't asking me directly, I stayed silent and waited for more to come. 'And you know my boss had this conversation with me about how fast I work a few weeks ago, and now I feel like I am being watched all the time. It makes me so stressed and then I get even more wrong. I just wish I was better at things. If I lose my job, bang go my chances of finding anywhere else to live.' She paused and let out a long breath, visibly calmer now in her body, although she looked bewildered and lost.

Not for the first time I could feel myself wanting to be her cheerleader. Here she was, 18 years of success and commitment in the same job, which, with her naturally empathic and warm style, she seemed so well suited to. And now, suddenly, she was feeling like she was failing. I smiled at her. 'I can feel myself wanting to say things to build you up and champion you,' I told her, 'And I wonder why I feel drawn to do that.'

'I need building up! Go for it!' Sylvia pleaded, half seriously.

'What do you need, do you think? What would "building you up" feel like?'

She sighed. 'I just want someone to tell me I am doing a good job, like I'm okay as I am, you know, and to feel supported and confident, not nervous and second-guessing myself.'

I let this sit between us for a little while.

'Do you feel you are – doing a good job, I mean?'

'Yes,' she said emphatically.

I wondered why knowing that for herself wasn't enough, why she needed to hear this from me, or anyone else. As I began to say this, going carefully, Sylvia's face crumpled and tears came to her eyes. I stopped and waited a while for her to feel whatever was coming. She continued to hold my gaze and nodded, tears flowing freely now, and reached for the tissues on the table next to her. No words were said between us, but I felt I understood something new. Once her tears had subsided, she said: 'She did that for me, you know?' I did know, now. 'In that moment just now, as you were asking me why I needed you to say to me, it felt like I lost Nicky all over again. Honestly, I felt it right in my stomach here,' She pushed a fist into her stomach. 'She's always done that– given me confidence, advice, made me feel good about myself. Without her, I have to do it myself, don't I?

'What I heard you say is that your need for emotional connection was always met by your friend Nicky, not by your parents or family maybe?' I confirmed.

'Yeah, we don't do emotions in our family,' she said with a dry laugh.

We both paused, and I took a breath in. 'Yeah, I see. And how are you doing right now?'

'I feel scared. I mean, I don't know how to do this myself and I don't want to. She should be here!'

Twentieth-century theories about grief were mostly based on the idea that, in order to resolve grief, people must 'let go and move on'. Research emerging from several studies in the 1990s led to an alternative paradigm, which has retained credibility and popularity ever since. It was based on the idea that, by establishing 'continuing bonds' with the person who has died, we are enabled to live better with our loss. It is a way of acknowledging that we have a continuing relationship with the dead (Klass et al., 2014), and celebrates that. It is the basis of the sensible idea that we don't 'recover' from grief; we are changed irrevocably by the loss we experience but we live with that loss, carrying it with us. We don't have to 'get over it and move on'. I wanted to help connect Sylvia to Nicky, to hear perhaps her internalised voice and feel her regulating presence in her life now.

'You're scared and it sounds like you are also angry?'

'Yeah, I am. I have to do this for everyone else, don't I – make them feel okay and help them when they are trying to work through arguments or problems. I'd just like someone to do that for me, and the one, lovely person who supported me has gone. It's not fair.'

'If Nicky was here, listening,' I stretched my upturned palms out towards Sylvia, carefully trying to invoke Nicky in the room between us, 'how would she feel? What would she say?'

Sylvia considered this and the suddenly her eyes lit up. 'Aaaah, I see what you are saying'.

'Could you hold that thought for a moment and try to feel what comes?' I said. 'Humour me,' I gently teased.

She closed her eyes: 'Okay, yeah, I can see her face clearly and what comes to me straight away is that she would be angry with me for feeling angry that she has gone. She would tell me to get a grip and just go back to work tomorrow and keep being me and if I lose my job, it's their loss and it probably meant it was time to leave anyway. Tough love, you know, that's her thing.' Her eyes opened again.

'Anything more?' I asked.

'She'd like you, that's for sure.' We both laughed at this and then she dropped her voice and finished with, 'And she'd say I'll be okay.'

After this session we had a break of a few weeks as Sylvia had finally found a new house and was preoccupied with moving, and needed some time off to focus on that. In that time the world changed with the arrival of the global Covid pandemic. Meeting face to face for therapy was no longer possible and we began to meet online, which we continued to do until the end of our work together. In our first online session, once we'd establish video and audio contact and got over the business of managing the technology, Sylvia put her hand up, a serious look on her face.

'I have to start by telling you something. It's huge for me.'

'Please do,' I replied, our turn-taking a little stilted due to internet bandwidth issues.

'What you said to me about Nicky, that moment from our last session, I literally can't stop thinking about it. Now, when I look at her picture, I can see her smiling and I can feel she is with me all the time, instead of it being so painful. And at work, that's actually a really long story I'll tell you about that later, but if anything goes wrong, I just can hear her voice in my head. And, even better, when my mum is on the phone going on at me about this and that, instead of getting angry or upset, I can see Nicky winking at me. She always had the measure of my mum.' She sat back, smiling.

'Sylvia, first I am so pleased to hear that, that sounds so powerful. But I didn't do that, you did. It was the moment that you realised what she meant for you that unlocked all of that.'

'Yes, I suppose.'

'Yes.'

'But I am, you know.' She stumbled a little on her words: 'I am and I want you to know I feel grateful to you.'

'I can hear that, and I so enjoyed hearing how much you've taken from it. That's what this process is all about. I just want to reflect back to you that this is work that *you are doing* – we are doing it together, if you like.'

'Okay, yeah, I'll take that,' she replied.

As we move into midlife and beyond, we are also relying on cues and clues from our own parents about how life should and could be. Exploring how this impacts our own experience can be liberating and provide a map for us. Julia Cameron, author of the groundbreaking book on creativity, *The Artist's Way* (1995), talks to the host of the podcast 'The Shift' about her own midlife transition as a time of 'enforced introspection' that we should succumb to (Baker, 2022). This heavily resonated with me when I heard it, as my own experience has been similar. The Covid pandemic, for many reasons, brought about the end of Sylvia's much-loved job at the GP practice, but due to a decent- sized redundancy payout, she was able to take some time to take stock herself. Our work quickly became focused on who she wanted to be at this next stage of her life, specifically on her resolution of *not* becoming her mother.

'I've been thinking about what job I am going to do next, although I love not working. I don't have a choice. And I really feel now that I want to do something with meaning, something that helps other people.'

I was concerned that Sylvia might still feel the need to make others feel okay, which had been her role in the family her whole life. I checked this out with her, asked her to explore it some more.

'No, it's different now. It isn't because I need everyone to think I am nice, kind of keep the peace. I just really don't want to be resentful and demanding as I get older. You know Darren lives nearby now and he has asked me to look after his two little ones after nursery one day a week. I could say no, I need to work after all, but I don't want to say no. These are my grandchildren; I want to know them, and I want them to know me.'

'Ah, so this is a helping act that helps you too, gives you something?' I asked.

'It gives me everything really, this big family. I can either see it as a long list of people needing stuff from me or too busy with their own lives to call me, or I can see it as a long list of people who I get to hang out with. I just don't want to resent them.'

'I see,' I replied.

Sylvia surprised me with what came next. She looked shy and uncertain and then said, 'I wondered what you thought of me applying for a job in a care home?' She was almost wincing in preparation for my reply.

'Just before I answer that, what is happening for you? Your face looks concerned.'

'I just really want to apply but I am worried you will say it's a silly idea!'

'Because?'

'Then I might not apply for it, and I'm actually really excited by it.'

'So, if I have this right, you are excited by the prospect of this new job and you want to apply but you are checking it out with me in case it is a silly idea.'

'No, I know it isn't a silly idea.'

'So, what's really happening here?'

'I think I need you to say "Go for it".'

I waited to see if anything else came.

'You're right,' she said. 'I don't need you to say that – I sent off the application yesterday.'

'And I am glad,' I said with a grin. 'Can you tell me more about it?'

It was an events and outings coordinator job at her local care home, working five mornings a week, which gave her time to help look after her grandchildren. For what it's worth, I did think she would be brilliant at it. Clearly the management at the home did too, and they gave her the job. This proved to be fortuitous as her mother was given a terminal diagnosis shortly after Sylvia started her new job. Sylvia surprised both of us by moving her mother into her own home and choosing to care for her until she died a few months later.

As I write this chapter, I notice my inclination to write the whole story of my time with Sylvia, and all of her story. In the other chapters, I've only drawn on snippets of client experiences. I think it has to do with the nature of the work we did together. Sylvia was going back over her own story and her family story to resolve something for herself: who was she, who did she want to be as she entered her next decade? As we age and the next generation becomes more dependent on us for support, inevitably this changing dynamic brings up patterns from our past, even for those of us with the most functional of childhoods. Crucially, Sylvia wanted to make sure she didn't blindly repeat the patterns of the past and find herself becoming like her mother.

Ageing theory believes that it is through the telling of stories and reviewing and reminiscing about our life that we can understand our history and age in an empowered and rich way (Bohlmeijer et al., 2007; Wong & Watt, 1991). Identity theorists, the most influential of these being Judith Butler, go further to say that, by telling our stories, we increase our self-referent knowledge and deepen our own identity (Butler, 1989). In psychotherapy, Gestalt theory also encourages storytelling as a means of experiencing feelings in the present moment and resolving unfinished business from the past. Recalling stories is not enough; retelling and feeling into the memory of them, reliving and resolving our stories, can free us up for a new way of being. So maybe that's the explanation for my urge to say more.

What has become apparent from my work with people at the time of their midlife transition is that it can cause us to relive past experiences or re-awaken patterned behaviours from the past. For example, the declining health of our parents may remind us of difficult times in our family, or grudges we may hold against siblings, or we may be experiencing losses and changes in adult friendship groups that remind us of difficult times with friends at school or places where we didn't fit in earlier in our lives. Equally, it is a time when, for people of all genders, our hormones and bodies change rapidly – a reversal of the process of our pubescent years – and this can bring forth echoes of the past and our experience of that first of all transitions. In the therapeutic space, it is helpful to be curious and alive to this possibility. For example, research has shown that adverse childhood experiences (ACEs) and early trauma may put women at higher risk of depression during menopause (Epperson et al., 2017). How we have transitioned throughout life – child to adult and thence to parent – holds clues that may be powerful to us now; if we explore them and build our self-awareness, we can approach each subsequent transition with this insight.

Grace, a marketing manager in her early 50s, had a relatively symptom-free menopause transition for the most part. 'I kind of got on with things,' she told me. 'I've faced a lot of tough times in my life; this didn't feel any harder than those. I went into it with my eyes open but I didn't suffer too badly actually.' She chose not to take HRT, due to her mild symptoms. The only thing she noticed was her weight creeping up in 'all the usual places'. Grace was active; she ran and weight trained frequently; she had been a professional field athlete in her late teens and early 20s, so she was used to her body feeling strong and lithe. She described how this shift in her weight very quickly gave way to what she called 'old, unhelpful behaviours'. When she gave up her beloved sports in her 20s and found herself facing a crisis of identity, the controlled eating patterns that had been helpful and healthy began to become disordered as she struggled to find her way into a new career and persona. 'I couldn't believe a grown, professional woman could end up with an eating disorder,' she told me, 'but I contacted my old support group and found a new sponsor to support me and that has been helping.'

In their awareness-raising work, The Menopause Charity in the UK clearly and helpfully highlights the connection between the menopause and eating disorders in an article on their website (Hodson, 2023):

> We know that many women will experience a resurgence of symptoms and behaviours during the menopause or even develop an eating disorder for the first time… [These are] often exacerbated by feelings of loss of control, anxiety, low mood, loss of motivation, of being overwhelmed and these are all common symptoms of the menopause.

This resurgence of responses from earlier in life can be confusing and distressing for people. As therapists, we can support clients by grounding them in the here and now, but recognising what belongs to the present and what needs to be resolved from the past in order for them to move forward. For Grace, this was simple – reconnecting with the specialist supportive eating disorder community helped her navigate this experience quite quickly.

The teenage person can be present in the midlife person in ways they might not immediately understand. A boy who was bullied as a teenager for being small and weak and coming late to puberty, who may have compensated by building muscle and training hard to excel at sport, may find himself challenged by the changes to his strength and stature, both physically and emotionally, during midlife. This may trigger feelings of inadequacy and fears of rejection, buried deep in past experiences. Noticing the use of language, body language and ways of relating within the therapeutic space and relationship can help to unearth this.

Susie, a client who I briefly worked with around the beginning of her menopause journey, told me that she was someone who never wanted to show weakness. She was the youngest of three siblings, the only girl, and her older brothers teased her mercilessly as she began to go through puberty. Part of her currency in the family, which she took into the world of school, college and work, was to be invincible, capable and never to show weakness. 'Yeah, this is definitely part of my process,' she had told me, rolling her eyes in recognition. 'While I loved being a mum when my children were born, once I returned to my job, I felt reluctant to let it affect my work.' Susie was a senior nurse in oncology. 'I help others for a living, I am supposed to have this sorted!' she said. 'I feel, rightly or wrongly, that these experiences of being a woman, of hormonal and physical changes, could be a sign of weakness. I feel I want to push against it, I want to be the best version of myself.' Recognising this pattern in her embodied experience in the world seemed helpful to Susie, in as much as she was then able to notice when a younger part of herself was present, particularly when her menopause symptoms made her feel vulnerable and she was trying to fight against them. I think it allowed her to craft a path between vulnerability and strength and find some acceptance of herself in the times when she felt less than invincible.

Allowing space for reviewing the life lived by clients and listening in for deeply embedded patterns or narratives like this can help make sense of how they are travelling into major life transitions. This became especially vibrant and important when Sylvia's mother moved in for the final weeks leading up to her death. Sylvia was struggling with sleep; her mother needed helping to the toilet every few hours, even through the night. 'It's like the worst days of my menopause before I started on HRT,' she joked. 'I feel like I am floating through the days in a haze.' She was, however, very curious about why, even in the depths of the night with no sleep, as she struggled to support her mother onto the commode, she felt nothing but an outpouring of compassion. 'My mother hated kindness, hated it, when we were growing up. You know, she had four girls in a tiny house, and I think she was bitter as hell. I remember other women from where we lived popping in, asking if she needed anything – that was the way then. When they left, she would talk about them, unkindly sometimes, and she'd tell us all about what she'd heard about them. I just remember her muttering and banging around.' She stopped here, lost in thought. 'I mean, that's a horrible early memory to have of your mum, isn't it? Other people seem to remember sunshine, cuddles and laughter!'

'*Your* mum?' I repeated her phrase back to her for emphasis.

She laughed ironically, '*My* mum'.

'Why did you switch out 'my' for 'your?'

'I think deep down I've always been so embarrassed and ashamed of her. She never had a good word to say about people – about us even. She doesn't seem to have it in her to do that.' She went on to tell me the many times, such as when she got her school-leaving certificate and when she married for the first time, that her mum seemed almost angry, definitely critical and always vocal about what wasn't being done right.

I remember being struck by sadness as she reminisced; it felt like a deep pull in my abdomen. It was fleeting but it was there, and I shared it with Sylvia. I wondered if it was her sadness I was feeling, or my compassion for her experience.

'I think, now I'm talking about it, perhaps she was just sad. I don't know how happy her life was. She'd have to be sad, wouldn't she, to behave like that all the time?' Sylvia mused.

'Hmm, maybe,' I said, and waited.

'And I've just realised that's how she was all my life, although it is kind of awful when I say it back, and that's what made me kind of resolute not to be like that.' She sat back in her chair a little and sighed a small 'Huh.'

'Huh?' I encouraged her to say more.

'Well, it's good, isn't it? I always thought of myself as a doormat, doing everything for everyone and not putting myself first. Oh my goodness, all the times I have talked about that here and thought I must have such a low opinion of myself. What if I am like this because I want to not be like her? Like looking after her now, this is something she would never do. But I can, and I am. In spite of her.'

I remember I felt a lifting in my body; I think it was hope. I felt Sylvia was right on the cusp of an awareness, and I didn't want to come crashing in. I stayed silent, just nodding to show I'd heard.

'So, you know, when I go to her in the night,' Sylvia continued 'and I am fighting with her to get her upright and out of bed, and she's telling me I'm doing it all wrong and shouting at me about this and that, I can just think "Well, I am being kind, anyway, and that's okay with me".' She stopped, satisfied, 'Yeah, that's okay with me. That's who I am.'

In her sweeping and comprehensive study of women, psychoanalyst and existential philosopher Simone de Beauvoir talks in mostly pessimistic terms about middle-age. Not for her the positive psychology of the second half of the 20th century. Written in 1949, as a reaction to the powerfully male-centred psychoanalytical theory originated by Freud, *The Second Sex* is undoubtedly dated in its outlook, but something important prevails, nevertheless. Wrapped within existential principles of the gritty reality of existence and the inevitable limitations of our embodied life, there is a call for women to find freedom as they age and to be more than what modern life has demanded of them. De Beauvoir writes (1949/1988):

> Now she becomes a different being, unsexed but complete: an old woman… When she has given up the struggle against the fatality of time, another combat begins: she must maintain a place on earth. (p.595)

Perhaps the coming into ourselves at this potent time of life, with children growing into adults, parents retreating into dependency and fertility no longer holding us, is more than the shuffling of the generations; perhaps it is the first moment when we can be free to own our existence and identity, unencumbered. Certainly, hearing Sylvia begin to be comfortable with who she was in relation to her mother's criticisms and in reaction to the profound loss of her friend, I had a strong sense of her settling into herself, with a radical acceptance of who she was.

And this radical acceptance of who we are can be ignited via the counselling relationship. When people come to counselling, they must feel that they are in a space that is free from assumptions and prejudice and rich with gentle curiosity, a space where each part of them can be encouraged and seen in all its glory. Novelist and activist Anne Lamott talks triumphantly about this process in her writing. Her reflections on her own ageing are that it has allowed her to become the woman she always wanted to be but didn't dare to hope for (2006). Ageing well, and finding growth as we age, can come through retelling our life stories, and those of other generations, and finding meaning and acceptance within them. Such a process helps clients like Sylvia move up through the branches of their family tree to occupy their new roles with intent and choice. As I wrote in my own book on ageing well (Kewell, 2019):

> This process is part of attaining wisdom, of locating oneself within time and within generations. It is also a powerful rebellion against the stories that other people tell us. Telling stories, and having them listened to, is a wonderful way of celebrating and retaining our own, unique identity. So, sit, be curious and listen as these stories are told and retold. (p.154)

Chapter 9
A midlife manifesto

…for me the vanishing of youthful, sometimes tyrannical, passions has made me appreciate the starry skies more and all wonders of being alive, wonders that I had previously overlooked… I've never felt better or more at peace with myself.
Irvin D. Yalom, *Creatures of a Day* (2015, p.48)

Most life transitions – puberty, parenthood, leaving school, changing career – carry the spark of something new. However, our later life transitions – retirement, menopause, children leaving the family home – are mostly characterised by a sense of loss or lessening. My aim in writing this book was to highlight not only how the midlife shift can impact our emotional landscape and mental wellbeing, and how this can be worked with in counselling, but also to rip open the curtains to explore what can be new, additive and exciting about it – to show the possibilities of midlife, of where it can take us. For psychotherapists and counsellors, in our practice and as individuals, holding the potential for this possibility creates the space for exactly that to happen. I hope that reading these pages has helped you in some way, whatever your role or perspective.

There are so many portrayals of midlife that focus on deficit. Advertisers of anti-ageing products promise to restore us to our former selves, and at their worst encourage fear of ageing and irrelevance. Literature is rife with people who are struggling to locate themselves and find meaning in the bleak landscape of our middle years – most notably, Arthur Miller's play *Death of a Salesman* (1949/2015) and works such as Eugene O'Neill's *The Iceman Cometh* (1939/1994), *Therapy* by David Lodge (2011), the funny but poignant *The Woman Who Went to Bed for a Year* by Sue Townsend (2012), and so many more. A zillion research studies and self-help guides rightly focus on women's negative and profoundly distressing experiences of the menopause and our failures, in the Western industrialised world at least, to take proper care of menopausal women in the workplace. Even as I write this in 2023, yet another study emerges showing how they struggle to find work environments that acknowledge and accommodate their physical and psychological needs (Department of Health & Social Care, 2022) and get adequate help from our medical system (Cleghorn, 2021). Germaine Greer was writing about these very same issues 30 years ago in *The Change* (1991/2018), her sweeping manifesto for a better experience of midlife for women.

I would argue, with many others, that we are wrong to focus exclusively on the negatives of midlife, and my hope is that some of the stories in this book show how this balance of crisis and growth plays out in each individual life. In 2011, ageing expert and psychologist Laura Carstensen published a groundbreaking longitudinal study into happiness, as part of her wider research work on longevity. This is her argument too: that middle age, far from being a time of deficit, is a time when we are uniquely capable, resilient and resourceful. Furthermore, we begin to be happier and more fulfilled the older we get. It is a radically different view, but it is underpinned by solid, long-term research into life-span development from the University of Geneva. From her review of the evidence, Carstensen concludes with what for me is the most powerful fact: 'Midlife is a time when cognition and emotion blend optimally in ways that give people insights into themselves and others.' If this isn't a manifesto for self-reflection and growth in our middle years, then I honestly don't know what is.

Where does counselling fit in? Some would argue that, by promoting counselling in midlife, I am suggesting we are indeed in crisis. Not so. And this perspective is borne out in the many accounts in this book. Across the years I have been practising, I have met and worked with many people who have come to see me for a vast array of issues and, as we begin the process of reflection, an unfolding has taken place – a growth orientation towards something latent but not yet realised. In the early years of my training, I was greatly impacted by a book I found by chance while trawling through the library shelves. The name of the book, *The Heroic Client* (Duncan et al., 2004), was bold and provocative. It's 20 years old now, but the ideas still hold true. Its authors, Barry Duncan, Scott Miller and Jacqueline Sparks, challenge traditional therapy's focus on analysis or direction, and the idea of a knowing or guiding therapist. They advocate instead that we harness our clients' innate capacity to regenerate, making therapy a collaborative partnership between empowered clients and accountable therapists. Clients are the heroes and heroines of their own therapeutic journeys. It has its roots, of course, in Rogers' and Maslow's conceptualisations of humans as growth orientated. What I took from reading this book was the idea that we should honour the internal and external dialogue of the person who has come to counselling, and trust that, deep down, they know where their areas for growth are. I believe that it is within the safety of the therapy relationship that the direction towards growth is co-created.

You will have read in Chapter 1 how Jane, coming for help to manage her chronic ill health, found herself surprised and angry at how dependable and helpful she had been throughout her life, and left counselling with new plans for semi-retirement, excited about what the future might bring. In 'Putting On a Show', we met Andrew, physically strong but seeking counselling when physical pain was bringing him down. The process of counselling over the next two years took us through his whole life span and many traumas, on a healing journey that brought together other versions of who he was to form a stronger, more valued current sense of self – one that believed he deserved love and all the good things the second half of his life might bring.

In researching this book, I spoke to countless people. I feel privileged that so many trusted me with their stories. The overall message I am left with is that the second half of life can have a different energy, meaning and pace than the first. It can happen *to* us, or it can happen *with* us. If we lean into it, notice what is happening and use our resources, we have the opportunity to be truly alongside our midlife journey, by which I mean to be experiencing it fully and finding meaning in what is happening, even if it is painful or distressing, as it so often can be. And this is true for all of us, not just those who come into therapy.

Right at the start of my research, I spoke with Sarah, a retail consultant in her late 40s. She told me how she noticed a pull inward, inside of herself, at a time when life was very much drawing her outwards and in many directions. Her job was at its most busy, she was making a life with a new partner, a newly blended family with teenage children. They were all moving between two households. 'I have an auto-immune condition,' she told me, 'so I live with discomfort within my body every day, but something about the onset of my menopause meant I became a much better observer of myself. As each symptom arrives, I try to be curious about what it is, what I might need to do to support it. I try to be patient!' Sarah went on to explain that she also lived with the fear that what she was experiencing – crippling insomnia, anxiety and tearfulness at work and periods of feeling dark and despairing – might overpower her ability to work.

Having always run her own business, Sarah was passionately independent and proud of it; it was devastating for her to think that her career might be at risk. Sarah explained that she knew from living with chronic pain that fighting it would do little to help, so instead she tried to listen inward to decide what adjustments she wanted or needed to make to her life or work in order to live well through this transition. 'In some ways it is easy for me to do this precisely because I have worked for myself for all this time, I am used to negotiating things in a way that works for me,' she told me.

Sarah had always had a keen sense of adventure; travel was a passion and she had worked and lived in many countries. She told me that she had always thought of herself as a sensitive person, open and curious to what was around her and within her at each life transition, such as becoming a mother or moving countries. 'My transitions are a chance to reinvent myself – I almost welcome them and always want to prepare for them and understand what is happening.' Sarah engaged early in a dialogue with her doctor, sought help proactively through occupational therapy and personal reflection, and introduced new self-care practices. The result? 'Well, it was a bit of a surprise, but I felt that I wanted to be less visible at work, not so much to be leading projects or being "the expert" on something, and I have moved naturally into a role where I facilitate connections between others to get the job done or create an output. I feel like I want to grow and connect outwards rather than drive forwards or upwards. It is quite liberating.' This same curiosity and reinvention led Sarah to take up a new hobby – singing in a local choir – and to start studying again. I felt, in talking to her, that amid the pain and uncertainty of the menopause itself, she had created a stronger, renewed sense of identity.

Another of my conversations stood out most poignantly because the environment so beautifully mirrored its meaning. I was talking to Yvonne, who described herself as 'peri-perimenopausal… on the fringes'. A Forest School teacher, working with early-years children in the natural environment, she spent much of her time outdoors and had a strong connection with nature. 'I am intrigued at the shift within myself from fertile to not fertile. In the holding (and fertile) space of mother nature where I spend so much of my time, I want to listen to change that is happening, and I'm curious about how it will leave me,' she told me. Yvonne, admittedly, wasn't experiencing any obvious symptoms but she was turning towards her perimenopause consciously and with intent, hoping to access her connection to nature to support and guide her.

More than that, Yvonne felt excited at the prospect of what she called 'permissive change'. 'It's like I have permission to struggle and to be different. I suppose it is quite nice and empowering to be able to be different. It's a form of release.' We had our conversation in nature, naturally. It was October, we were wrapped in warm clothes and wearing sturdy shoes, and we wandered through the woods near to where Yvonne lived, drops from a recent shower falling from naked trees, the ground thick with layers of glossy brown leaves. As we carefully stepped over a tree trunk, Yvonne paused and crouched down. 'Do you see all these mushrooms popping up all over this trunk? They weren't here a couple of days ago,' she said, and ran her fingers gently over tiny hoods of brown and white. 'I suppose I see my approaching menopause in the same way. One day it will be here fully, and it might not be pretty, but it will have blossomed up anyway and it will demand my attention, just like these.' This image has stayed with me; it seemed to suggest an innate curiosity and desire to connect to something beyond the body and our own self.

I am offering this perspective to invite practitioners, anyone reading this indeed, to see through the caricatures and stereotypes to the emerging possibilities unfolding in front of us; to see through the crisis to find the potential for growth within us; to get in front of, or at least get even with, life events and imbue them with meaning; to find a purpose to navigate towards. As I've explained, I am a humanistic, existential counsellor. My counselling modality has its roots in philosophy and takes a curious and courageous approach to unearthing meaning and purpose in people's lives. It uses the therapeutic encounter – two individuals interacting in a therapeutic relationship – as a way to help people get closer to their true selves. It is founded on the belief that none of us really 'know'; the therapist comes into that encounter as a fallible human being and guides the process of discovery through interaction. *The Wiley World Handbook of Existential Therapy* describes this brilliantly as 'a mutual, collaborative, encouraging dialogue between two struggling human beings' (van Deurzen et al., 2019, p.3). Researchers into midlife psychological development would agree with this; even studies from 50 years ago, on which much of our social policy is still based, conclude that, in later stages of life, people are seeking connection and purpose as well as guidance and encouragement (Neugarten, 1968). Germaine Greer mentions in *The Change* that there are few leaders 'beckoning' us all towards how it should be (1991/2018). So, it is up to all of us to find the map of the territory and look to the guiding star within ourselves to find our way. To my mind, counselling helps us do this. It is my hope that the stories in this book have shown that to be true.

References

Accius, J. & Joo Yeoun, S. (2019). *The longevity economy outlook: How people aged 50 and older are fueling economic growth, stimulating jobs, and creating opportunities for all.* AARP Thought Leadership.

Alighieri, D. (c.1321/2009). *The divine comedy of Dante Alighieri. Volume 1: Inferno* (Trans. S. Lombardo). Hackett Classics.

Anderson, D. & Posner, N. (2002). Relationship between psychosocial factors and health behaviours for women experiencing menopause. *International Journal of Nursing Practice, 8*(5), 265–273. https://doi.org/10.1046/j.1440-172X.2002.00376.x

Appignanesi, L. (2008). *Mad, bad and sad: A history of women and the mind doctors from 1800 to the present.* Virago.

Applewhite, A. (2017, April). *Let's end ageism.* TED Talk. www.ted.com/talks/ashton_applewhite_let_s_end_ageism

Baker, S. (2020). *The shift: How I (lost and) found myself after 40 – and you can too.* Coronet.

Baker, S. (Speaker). (2022). *Julia Cameron on alcoholism, creativity and emotional sobriety.* [Audio podcast]. The Shift with Sam Baker. https://podcasts.apple.com/es/podcast/julia-cameron-on-alcoholism-creativity-and-emotional/id1527442768?i=1000574709720

Balance (2021, October 21). *Menopause symptoms are killing women's careers, major survey reveals.* [Blog.] Newson Health. www.balance-menopause.com/news/menopause-symptoms-are-killing-womens-careers-major-survey-reveals/

Barr, N. (2007, September). Nikki Giovanni's Aha! Moment. *O: The Oprah Magazine.* www.oprah.com/spirit/nikki-giovannis-aha-moment

Berman, A.L. & McNelis, K. (2017). *Help-seeking among men: Implications for suicide prevention.* Centre for Suicide Prevention. https://www.suicideinfo.ca/resource/help-seeking-among-men-implications-for-suicide-prevention

Birmingham, B. (2021). *Middle-aged women rock: A menopause story for a new generation*. Orlay Kelly.

Blackie, S. (2022). *Hagitude: Reimagining the second half of life*. September Publishing.

Bodza, C., Morrey, T. & Hogan, K.F. (2019). How do counsellors having menopausal symptoms experience their client work: An interpretative phenomenological analysis. *Counselling & Psychotherapy Research, 19*, 544–552. https://doi.org/10.1002/capr.12231

Bohlmeijer, E., Roemer, M., Cuijpers, P. & Smit, F. (2007). The effects of reminiscence on psychological well-being in older adults: A meta-analysis. *Aging & Mental Health, 11*(3), 291–300. doi: 10.1080/13607860600963547

Bott, D. & Howard, P. (2012). *The therapeutic encounter: A cross-modality approach*. Sage.

Bronfenbrenner, U. (1993). Ecological models of human development. In M. Gauvain & M. Cole (Eds.), *Readings on the development of children*. Freeman (pp.37–43).

Brown, S.L. & Wright, M.R. (2019). Divorce attitudes among older adults: Two decades of change. *Journal of Family Issues, 40*(8), 1018–1037. https://doi.org/10.1177/0192513X19832936

Buber, M. (1923/2023). *I and thou*, Scribner.

BUPA. (2022). Written evidence from BUPA. UK Parliament. https://committees.parliament.uk/writtenevidence/39244/pdf/

Butler, J.P. (1990). *Gender trouble: Feminism and the subversion of identity*. Routledge.

Butler, O. (1993). *Parable of the sower*. Headline Publishing Group.

Cameron, J. (1995). T*he artist's way: A course in discovering and recovering your creative self*. Pan Books.

Candy, L. (2023, June 11). 'I started to unravel': Why do so many women over 40 struggle with stress? *The Guardian*. www.theguardian.com/lifeandstyle/2023/jun/11/i-started-to-unravel-why-do-so-many-women-over-40-struggle-with-stress

Carreira, H., Williams, R., Müller, M., Harewood, R., Stanway, S. & Bhaskaran, K. (2018). Associations between breast cancer survivorship and adverse mental health outcomes: A systematic review. *Journal of the National Cancer Institute, 110*(12), 1311–1327. https://doi.org/10.1093/jnci/djy177

Carstensen, L. (2011). *A long bright future*. Broadway Books.

Centre for Ageing Better. (2022). *Work: The state of ageing 2022*. Centre for Ageing Better. https://ageing-better.org.uk/work-state-ageing-2022

CIPD. (2022). *Understanding older workers: Analysis and recommendations to support longer and more fulfilling working lives.* CIPD. https://www.cipd.org/globalassets/media/knowledge/knowledge-hub/reports/understanding-older-workers-report_tcm18-107672.pdf

Cleghorn, E. (2021). *Unwell women: A journey through medicine and myth in a man-made world*. Weidenfeld & Nicolson.

Cooper, M. (2003). *Existential psychologies*. Sage.

Cooper, R. (2008). Prime time: TV menopause, queerly a case for review. *SQS–Suomen Queer-tutkimuksen Seuran lehti, 3*(2), 30–37.

Corinna, H. (2021). *What fresh hell is this? Perimenopause, menopause, other indignities and you*. Piatkus.

Cox, L. (2017). *Here we are: Feminism for the real word*. Algonquin Young Readers.

Criado Perez, C. (2020). *Invisible women: Exposing data bias in a world designed for men*. Vintage Books.

Dattani, S., Rodés-Guirao, L., Ritchie, H., Roser, M. & Ortiz-Ospina, E. (2023). *Suicides*. Our World In Data. https://ourworldindata.org/suicide

de Beauvoir, S. (1949/1988). *The second sex*. Picador.

de Beauvoir, S. (1970/1972). *Old age*. London: HarperCollins.

Degges-White, S. & Myers, J.E. (2006). Transitions, wellness, and life satisfaction: Implications for counseling midlife women. *Journal of Mental Health Counseling, 28*(2), 133–150.

Department of Health & Social Care. (2022, April 13). *Women's health strategy: Call for evidence*. https://www.gov.uk/government/consultations/womens-health-strategy-call-for-evidence/womens-health-strategy-call-for-evidence

Duncan, B.L., Miller, S.D. & Sparks, J.A. (2004). *The heroic client: A revolutionary way to improve effectiveness through client-directed, outcome-informed therapy*. Jossey-Bass Inc.

Epperson, C.N., Sammel, M.D., Bale, T.L., Kim, D.R., Conlin, S., Scalice, S., Freeman, K. & Freeman, E.W. (2017). Adverse childhood experiences and risk for first-episode major depression during the menopause transition. *Journal of Clinical Psychiatry, 78*(3), e298-e307.

Erikson, E.H. & Erikson, J.M (1998). *The life cycle completed* (Extended version). W.W. Norton & Co.

Fawcett Society. (2022). *Menopause and the workplace.* The Fawcett Society. www.fawcettsociety.org.uk/menopauseandtheworkplace

Feiler, B. (2021). *Life is in the transitions: Mastering change at any age.* Penguin Books.

Field, E., Krivkovich, A., Kügele, S., Robinson, N. & Yee, L. (2023, October 5). *Women in the workplace 2023.* McKinsey & Co. www.mckinsey.com/featured-insights/diversity-and-inclusion/women-in-the-workplace

Francis-Devine, B. & Hutton, G. (2024). *Women and the UK economy.* Research briefing. House of Commons Library. https://researchbriefings.files. parliament.uk/documents/SN06838/SN06838.pdf

Freud, S. (1925/1927). Some psychological consequences of the anatomical distinction between the sexes (Trans. J. Strachey). *International Journal of Psycho-Analysis, 8*(2), 133–142.

Gilleard, C. (2022). Aging as otherness: Revisiting Simone de Beauvoir's *Old Age. The Gerontologist, 62,(2),* 286–292. https://academic.oup.com/ gerontologist/article/62/2/286/6158979

Glyde, T. (2023). How can therapists and other healthcare practitioners best support and validate their queer menopausal clients? *Sexual and Relationship Therapy, 38*(4), 10.1080/14681994.2021.1881770

Greer, G. (1991/2018). *The change: Women, ageing and the menopause.* Bloomsbury.

Griffiths, A., Ceausu, I., Depypere, H., Lambrinoudaki, I., Mueck, A., Pérez-López, F.R., van der Schouw, Y.T., Senturk, L.M., Simoncini, T., Stevenson, J.C., Stute, P. & Rees, M. (2016). EMAS recommendations for conditions in the workplace for menopausal women. *Maturitas, 85,* 79–81. https://www. sciencedirect.com/science/article/abs/pii/S0378512215008403

Griffiths, A., MacLennan, S. & Wong, Y.Y.V. (2010). *Women's experience of working through the menopause.* The Institute of Work, Health & Organisations.

Hasseldine, R. (2020). Uncovering the root cause of mother-daughter conflict. *Counselling Today, 62*(7), 46–50.

Heidegger, M. (1927/2010). *Being and time* (Trans. J. Stambaugh). SUNY Press.

Henry, K.E. (2015). *'A wrinkle in time': Growing old, or, a queer unbecoming.* [Video]. Honors thesis. Wesleyan University. https://doi.org/10.14418/ wes01.1.1691

Hodson, Z. (2023). *Eating disorders and menopause.* The Menopause Charity. https://www.themenopausecharity.org/2021/04/24/eating-disorders-and-menopause/

Hofmeier, S.M., Runfola, C.D., Sala, M., Gagne, D.A., Brownley, K.A. & Bulik, C.M. (2017). Body image, aging, and identity in women over 50: The Gender and Body Image (GABI) study. *Journal of Women and Aging, 29*(1), 3–14. doi:10.1080/08952841.2015.1065140

Hunter, M. & Rendall, H. (2007). Bio-psycho-socio-cultural perspectives on menopause. *Best Practice & Research in Clinical Obstetrics and Gynaecology, 21*(2), 261–274. doi:10.1016/j.bpobgyn.2006.11.001

Jackson, M. (2020, March 25). Life begins at 40: the demographic and cultural roots of the midlife crisis. 2019 Wilkins–Bernal–Medawar lecture. *The Royal Society, 74*(3). https://doi.org/10.1098/rsnr.2020.0008

Jaques, E. (1965/1970). Death and the midlife crisis. Republished in Jaques, E. (1970). *Work, creativity, and social justice.* Heinemann (pp.38–63).

Johns Hopkins Medicine. (2023). *Hysterectomy.* https://www.hopkinsmedicine. org/health/treatment-tests-and-therapies/hysterectomy

Kermode, M. (2022, June 19). Good Luck to You, Leo Grande review – Emma Thompson excels in stagey sex comedy. *The Guardian.* https://www. theguardian.com/film/2022/jun/19/good-luck-to-you-leo-grande-review-emma-thompson-excels-in-stagey-sex-comedy

Kewell, H. (2019). *Living well and dying well: Tales of counselling older people.* PCCS Books.

Kirkland-Handley, N. & Mitchell, D. (2005). Anxiety and engagement. In E. Van Deurzen & C. Arnold-Baker (Eds.), *Existential perspectives on human issues: A handbook for therapeutic practice* (pp.180–188). Palgrave Macmillan.

Klass, D., Silverman, P.R. & Nickman, S. (2014) *Continuing bonds: New understandings of grief.* Routledge.

Koffka, K. (1935/2014). *Principles of Gestalt psychology.* Mimesis International.

Kopenhager, T. & Guidozzi, F. (2015). Working women and the menopause. *Climacteric: The Journal of the International Menopause Society, 18*(3), 372–375. https://doi.org/10.3109/13697137.2015.1020483

Lacan, J. (1980). *Ecrits: A selection* (Trans. A. Sheridan). Tavistock Publications.

Lamott, A. (2006). *Plan B: Further thoughts on faith.* Riverprint Books.

Langer, E.J. (2010). *Counterclockwise: A proven way to think yourself younger.* Hodder & Stoughton.

Lehmann, C. (2001, July 20). Women psychiatrists still battle Freud's view of sexes. *Psychiatric News.* https://doi.org/10.1176/pn.36.14.0009

Leventhal, J.L. (2000). Management of libido problems in menopause. *The Permanente Journal, 4*(3), 29–34.

Lindsey, E. (2010). *Curating humanity's heritage.* TEDWomen. https://www.ted.com/talks/elizabeth_lindsey_curating_humanity_s_heritage

Lodge, D. (2011). *Therapy.* Vintage.

Madison G. (Ed.). (2014). *Theory and practice of focusing-oriented psychotherapy: Beyond the talking cure.* Jessica Kingsley Publishers.

Maslow, A.H. (1968). *Toward a psychology of being* (2nd ed.). Van Nostrand Reinhold.

Mearns, D. & Thorne, B. (2000). *Person-centred therapy today: New frontiers in theory and practice.* Sage.

Menopause Support. (2022). *Info.* https://menopausesupport.co.uk/?page_id=60%3E%20(accessed%20July%202022

Merleau-Ponty, M. (1945/2002). *Phenomenology of perception* (Trans. C. Smith). Routledge Classics.

Miller, A. (1949/2015). *Death of a salesman.* Penguin Modern Classics.

Mind. (2023). *Mental health facts and statistics.* Mind. https://www.mind.org.uk/information-support/types-of-mental-health-problems/mental-health-facts-and-statistics/

Moran C. (2020, July 4). The drugs and menopause. *The Times.* https://www.thetimes.co.uk/article/caitlin-moran-me-drugs-and-the-perimenopause-mpzn2cdh2

MUVS: The Museum of Contraception and Abortion. (2016, January 12). *The birth of hormone research: Sterilisation was believed bring about eternal youth.* https://muvs.org/en/museum/newsletter/2016-01-12-the-birth-of-hormone-research-sterilisation-was-believed-bring-about-eternal-youth/

Namazi, M., Sadeghi, R. & Behboodi Moghadam, Z. (2019). Social determinants of health in menopause: An integrative review. *International Journal of Women's Health, 11*, 637–647. https://doi.org/10.2147/IJWH.S228594

Neugarten, B.L. (Ed.). (1968). *Middle age and ageing.* University of Chicago Press.

Neugarten, B.L. & Hagestad, G.O. (1976). Age and the life course. In R. Binstock & E. Shanas (Eds.), *Handbook of aging and the social sciences* (pp.35–55). Van Nostrand Reinhold.

Newson, L. & Lewis, R. (2019) *Menopause at work: A survey to look at the impact of menopausal and perimenopausal symptoms upon women in the workplace.* Newson Health: Research and Education. www.nhmenopausesociety.org/wp-content/uploads/2022/01/Menopause-at-Work.pdf

Newson, L., Martins, M. & McCracken, J. (2022). *A guide to all things menopause if you've had breast cancer.* Balance Menopause Support. https://balance-menopause.com/uploads/2022/01/Breast-cancer-booklet.pdf

NHS. (2023). *Male menopause.* www.nhs.uk/conditions/male-menopause

NHS Inform. (2023a). *Sexual wellbeing, intimacy and menopause.* https://www.nhsinform.scot/healthy-living/womens-health/later-years-around-50-years-and-over/menopause-and-post-menopause-health/sexual-wellbeing-intimacy-and-menopause

NHS Inform. (2023b). *Early and premature menopause.* https://www.nhsinform.scot/healthy-living/womens-health/later-years-around-50-years-and-over/menopause-and-post-menopause-health/early-and-premature-menopause

North American Menopause Society. (2023). *Instant help for induced menopause.* www.menopause.org/for-women/menopauseflashes/menopause-symptoms-and-treatments/instant-help-for-induced-menopause

Nuffield Health. (2021, updated 2023). *Not just a women's problem: Improving menopause workplace policy and support.* Nuffield Health. www.nuffieldhealth.com/article/breaking-the-stigma-the-biggest-workplace-menopause-challenges-and-how-to-tackle-them

Office for National Statistics. (2021). *National life tables – life expectancy in the UK: 2018 to 2020.* ONS. www.ons.gov.uk/peoplepopulationandcommunity/birthsdeathsandmarriages/lifeexpectancies/bulletins/nationallifetablesunitedkingdom/2018to2020

Office for National Statistics. (ONS). (2022a, September 6). *Suicides in England and Wales: 2021 registrations.* ONS. www.ons.gov.uk/peoplepopulationandcommunity/birthsdeathsandmarriages/deaths/bulletins/suicidesintheunitedkingdom/2021registrations

Office for National Statistics. (2022b). *Past and projected period and cohort life tables: 2020-based, UK, 1981 to 2070.* ONS. https://www.ons.gov.uk/peoplepopulationandcommunity/birthsdeathsandmarriages/lifeexpectancies/bulletins/pastandprojecteddatafromtheperiodandcohortlifetables/2020baseduk1981to2070

O'Neill, E. (1939/1994). *The iceman cometh.* Nick Hern Books.

Perls, F.S. (1969). *Gestalt therapy verbatim.* The Gestalt Journal Press.

Plath, S. (1963/2001). *The bell jar.* Faber & Faber.

Quddoos, H. (2023) *Claiming my voice as a BAME therapist and 'extending my hand to the white Other'.* UKCP. https://www.psychotherapy.org.uk/news/claiming-my-voice-as-a-bame-therapist-and-extending-my-hand-to-the-white-other

Reeves, R.V. (2022). *Of boys and men: Why the modern male is struggling, why it matters and what to do about it.* Swift Press.

Reuben, D. (1969). *Everything you always wanted to know about sex* (*But were afraid to ask).* Bantam Books.

Rogers, C.R. (1951/2003). *Client-centred therapy.* Constable.

Rogers, C.R. (1961). *On becoming a person: A therapist's view of psychotherapy.* Houghton Mifflin.

Rossetti, C. (1895/2008). *Christina Rossetti: Poems and prose.* Oxford University Press.

Saga. (2023). *'Generation Experience': The UK's economic superpower. The economic contribution of the UK 50-plus population to UK society.* Saga. www.saga.co.uk/generation-experience

Salimi, M., Yazdkhasti, M., Mahmoodi, Z., Kabir, K., Mirabi, P. & Yazdkhasti, M. (2019). Effectiveness of a multi-dimensional group counseling program based on the GATHER approach on the quality of life in surgically menopausal women. *JMM: Journal of Menopausal Medicine, 25*(3), 130–141. https://doi.org/10.6118/jmm.19200

Samaritans. (2020). *Out of sight, out of mind: Why less-well off, middle-aged men don't get the support they need.* Samaritans. https://media.samaritans.org/documents/Samaritans_-_out_of_sight_out_of_mind_2020.pdf

Samuel, J. (2022). *Every family has a story: How to grow and move forward together.* Penguin Random House.

Sartre, J.P. (1956/2003). *Being and nothingness: An essay on phenomenological ontology* (Trans. H.E. Barnes). Routledge.

Schoenaker, D.A., Jackson, C.A., Rowlands, J.V. & Mishra, G.D. (2014). Socioeconomic position, lifestyle factors and age at natural menopause: A systematic review and meta-analyses of studies across six continents. *International Journal of Epidemiology, 43*(5), 1542–1562. https://doi.org/10.1093/ije/dyu094

Settersten, R.A. Jr., Gunhild O. & Hagestad. (1996). What's the latest? Cultural age deadlines for family transitions. *The Gerontologist, 36*(2), 178–188.

Shakespeare, W. (1623/1993). As you like it. In *The Complete Works of William Shakespeare.* Ramboro.

Sheehy, G. (1995). *New passages: Mapping your life across time.* Random House.

Sheehy, G. (1999). *Understanding men's passages: Discovering a new map of men's lives.* Ballantine Books.

Shpancer, N. (2019, December 29). Why so many are satisfied being childless by choice. *Psychology Today*. https://www.psychologytoday.com/us/blog/insight-therapy/201912/why-so-many-are-satisfied-being-childless-choice

Spinelli, E. (2006) *Tales of un-knowing: Therapeutic encounters from an existential perspective.* PCCS Books.

Spinelli, E. (2007) *Practicing existential therapy: The relational world.* Sage.

Statistica. (2023, May 4). *Average age at divorce in England and Wales 2000-2019, by gender.* Statistica. https://www.statista.com/statistics/290096/divorce-average-age-at-divorce-in-england-and-wales-by-gender/

Stern, D. (1985). *The interpersonal world of the infant: A view from psychoanalysis and developmental psychology.* Basic Books.

Stevenson, R.L. (1879/1915). *Travels with a donkey* and *An inland voyage.* Macmillan.

Sturgis, I. (2016, July 27) Surgical menopause linked to poor memory and early-onset dementia. *The Telegraph.* https://www.telegraph.co.uk/health-fitness/body/surgical-menopause-linked-to-poor-memory-and-early-onset-dementi/

Townsend, S. (2012). *The woman who went to bed for a year.* Penguin.

UK Government. (2022, April 13). *Women's health strategy: Call for evidence.* www.gov.uk/government/consultations/womens-health-strategy-call-for-evidence/womens-health-strategy-call-for-evidence

UK Parliament. (2022, July 28). *New report: MPs call for new menopause ambassador to keep women in the workplace.* Press release. https://committees.parliament.uk/committee/328/women-and-equalities-committee/news/172500/new-report-mps-call-for-new-menopause-ambassador-to-keep-women-in-the-workplace/

van Deurzen, E. (2002). Heidegger's challenge of authenticity. In S. du Plock (Ed). *Further existential challenges to psychotherapeutic theory and practice.* Society for Existential Analysis (pp.370–379).

van Deurzen, E. (2012). *Existential counselling and psychotherapy in practice* (3rd ed.). Sage.

van Deurzen, E., Craig, E., Längle, A., Schneider, K.J., Tantam, D. & du Plock, S. (2019). *The Wiley world handbook of existential therapy.* Wiley.

Whyte, D. (1994.) *The heart aroused: Poetry and the preservation of the soul.* Bantam Doubleday Dell Publishing Group.

Williams, R.D. & Clark, A.J. (2000). A qualitative study of women's hysterectomy experience. *Journal of Women's Health & Gender-based Medicine, 9*(Suppl. 2), S15–S25. https://doi.org/10.1089/152460900318731

Williams, T. (1947/2009). *A streetcar named Desire*. Penguin Classics.

Williams, T. (1959/2009). *Sweet bird of youth and other plays*. Penguin Classics.

Wilson, R.A. (1966). *Feminine forever*. M. Evans & Company.

Winnicott, D. (1971). *Playing and reality*. Tavistock Press.

Women and Equalities Committee. (2022). *Menopause and the workplace: First report of session 2022–23*. UK Parliament. https://publications.parliament.uk/pa/cm5803/cmselect/cmwomeq/91/report.html

Wong, P.T. & Watt, L.M. (1991). What types of reminiscence are associated with successful aging? *Psychology and Aging, 6*(2), 272–279. https://doi.org/10.1037/0882-7974.6.2.272

World Bank. (2020). *Life expectancy at birth, total (years) – European Union*. World Bank. https://data.worldbank.org/indicator/SP.DYN.LE00.IN?locations=EU

World Economic Forum. (2023, February 23). *Charted: How life expectancy is changing around the world*. World Economic Forum. https://www.weforum.org/agenda/2023/02/charted-how-life-expectancy-is-changing-around-the-world/

Yalom, I.D. (2011). *Staring at the sun: Overcoming the dread of death*. Piatkus.

Yalom, I.D. (2015). *Creatures of a day*. Piatkus.

Index

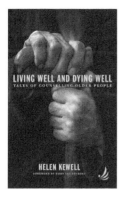

Living Well and Dying Well:
Tales of counselling older people
Helen Kewell (2019)

ISBNs:
pbk 978 1 910919 415
ebk 978 1 910919 736

Older people rarely feature in counselling literature, and the very old barely at all. Helen Kewell seeks to address this often overlooked topic with a vibrant collection of resonant case studies describing her encounters with some of the old and very old clients with whom she has worked as a counsellor. Woven into these accounts are her personal reflections on how working with these clients has changed her and contributed to her own growth as a counsellor and as a human being. She also describes the theoretical and philosophical works that have influenced her practice – looking to humanistic, existentialist and person-centred approaches to guide her in this largely uncharted territory.

Helen's aim in this book is to use story-telling about real people living real lives to inspire others to consider this work as possible, necessary and meaningful.

'*Helen's approach to counselling older adults is humanising, compassionate, and relationally deep. This unique text brings to life the reality and the potential of working with this client group. An invaluable read for counsellors and psychotherapists working in this field.*'
Mick Cooper, Professor of Counselling Psychology, University of Roehampton

Discounted prices and free UK delivery – www.pccs-books.co.uk